YESTERDAY'S PROPHETS

for Today's World

F. B. Huey, Jr.

Dewey Decimal Classification: 221.92

Subject heading: BIBLE. O.T. PROPHETS

Library of Congress Catalog Card Number: 79-54922

Printed in the United States of America

Preface

There is no greater area of continuing fascination in Old Testament studies than the prophets. They stand as mountain peaks of rugged grandeur in an otherwise all-too-bleak landscape that forms the story of Israel in the Old Testament. Scholars and preachers describe the faith of Israel in bold terms of self-sacrifice and stubborn commitment to God in spite of seemingly insurmountable obstacles. They exalt the stoic suffering and inspiring faithfulness of the Hebrew people.

However, they are not really describing the normal experiences of the people but are depicting the faith of those remarkable men called prophets. The history of the struggle of the Israelites to be a people pleasing to God has rightly been called a history of failure. The prophets who appeared in times of crisis were models of what God wanted all his people to be. They were the ones who voiced warning and gave direction to a nation that frequently lost its way.

These men are the subjects of study in this book. No other single group of people exercised so much influence in determining the faith of Israel—certainly not the priests, the kings, or wise men. When the prophets stood before the people and thundered, "Thus says the Lord," their audiences tried to ignore them. But they could not forget their words. They repeated to one another what these men of God had said. They passed on the stories to their children around the evening campfires and in their houses. Sooner or later someone wrote down their words, if the prophets themselves did not do it. In this way their words were preserved for future generations. After many centuries had passed, the messages of the prophets became enshrined among the sacred Scriptures of the Jewish people. In turn, the Jewish Scriptures were accepted as part of the Christian canon; so the prophets still speak today.

Though they exerted tremendous influence on the religious history of their people, the prophets still remain shrouded in mystery. They are the most misunderstood and frequently misused individuals in the Old Testament. In an age when it is popular to demolish heroes, some people treat the prophets as though there were nothing special about them. They even deny to them the ability to predict future events. For them the prophets were cranks and charlatans. They are represented as victims of self-deception about their ability to receive messages from God.

At the other extreme are those people who, though well-intentioned, exalt the prophets to superhuman, almost supernatural proportions. Their prophets emerge with glistening halos, crystal ball in hand, and thunderbolts up their sleeves to hurl at scoffers.

How, then, should the prophets be depicted? The answer is: Show them as they really were—both human and unique. To rob the prophets of their humanity and feet of clay is just as wrong as to deny them any endowment of divine power. An important lesson to come from a study of the prophets is that, though they were ordinary human beings like you and me, God spoke to them. He was able to communicate his will through them to his people. By acknowledging that the prophets were human beings, we can take heart that God is still in the business of turning the ordinary into the extraordinary. He can do it with everyday you-and-me kind of people, who otherwise may seem to have little potential for greatness.

The purpose of this book, then, is to examine various aspects of the prophets' experiences with the hope of arriving at a better understanding of these preachers of righteousness. What follows in these pages is really a reflection of my own continuing fascination with the prophets and desire to know them better. If the reader suddenly finds himself thinking of the prophet as a friend or someone he would like to know as he reads these pages, the book has accomplished its purpose. The encouragement for writing down these reflections on the prophets first came from students who were exposed to many of the ideas in classes and said they should be put in writing for a wider audience. Hopefully, their encouragement was not misplaced.

It should be made clear at the outset that this book was written for lay people and "nonprofessional" Bible students in language that will communicate to them. No apology is made for the simplicity of language and occasional repetition. There is too much biblical interpretation that reflects the effort of scholars to write for other scholars. What they have learned is all too rarely communicated to the great masses of Christians. The student in the pew is not immersed in technical terminology. He is unfamiliar with exegetical techniques of scholars, whose discussions appear obscure to him. He seldom benefits from the labors of great scholars, for they rarely tell him what they have learned in words he can understand. The scholar may find little that is new here, nevertheless he still may read some truths that speak to him in a fresh way.

In the chapters that follow, numerous references to Scriptures will be encountered that are not actually quoted. Though it will slow the reader, he should find the passages cited and read them for better comprehension of the topic being discussed. They were carefully chosen with that purpose in mind.

I do not claim to be a prophet or the son of a prophet. However, I believe I am safe in saying that long after this book is forgotten, people will continue to be fascinated by the Old Testament prophets and will still be trying to understand them. This statement is not made to acknowledge the inadequacy of the book but to recognize the complexity of the prophets and the unsearchable riches of the Word of God.

Contents

1

"Whom Shall I Send?"
(The Call of the Prophet)

The appropriate place to begin a study of an Old Testament prophet is with his call, for this was the event that ushered him into his prophetic office. Besides its appropriateness, there is no more fascinating study to be made in the Old Testament than that of the prophet's call. The divine encounter and the human response are dramatically depicted in the Bible when God called a man to be his spokesman.

Not every prophet's call is described in the Old Testament, but we assume that each was called. Each one in his unique fashion must have felt the hand of God upon him, compelling him to deliver God's message to his people. How else could we explain his faithfulness to a thankless and often unpleasant task? The messages of judgment he announced bore like a heavy weight about his neck. He took no delight in proclaiming the doom of his own people (Jer. 13:17; 23:9). Jeremiah (Jer. 23:33), Zechariah (Zech. 9:1; 12:1), and Malachi (Mal. 1:1) described the word of the Lord as a "burden." They felt the compulsive necessity of proclaiming God's word to Israel, even though at times they preferred not to speak. The prophet Amos felt this compulsion also and said, "The Sovereign LORD has spoken— who can but prophesy?" (Amos 3:8, NIV). Each of the prophets knew he had been called for the purpose of being God's spokesman. Therefore, he could not keep quiet.

When the account of a prophet's call is given in the Old Testament, we can profit by a careful study of it. The calls of Moses (Ex. 3:1 to 4:17), Samuel (1 Sam. 3), Isaiah (Isa. 6), Jeremiah (Jer. 1), and Ezekiel (Ezek. 1:1 to 3:15) are described in great detail. The calls of Abraham (Gen. 12:1-3),[1] Amos (Amos 7:14-15), Jonah (Jonah 1:1-2; 3:1-2), and Elisha (1 Kings 19:16,19-21) are described more briefly. The call of Hosea seems to have been linked with God's command to Beeri's son to get married (Hos. 1:2).

Nothing is said about the call of other prophets, unless it is implied in a phrase such as "the word of the Lord which came to . . ." (Joel 1:1; Mic. 1:1; Zeph. 1:1; Zech. 1:1). Similar statements include: "the word of the Lord came by the hand of . . ." (Hag. 1:1, literal translation); "the vision of . . ." (Nah. 1:1); "the oracle of God which Habakkuk the prophet saw" (Hab. 1:1); and "the burden of the word of the Lord to Israel through . . ." (Mal. 1:1). These enigmatic phrases probably reveal the conviction of the prophet that God had spoken to him and was saying, "Here is what I want you to say to your people."

There are other prophets who appear abruptly upon the scene without any mention of their initial call and commissioning by God. They include Elijah the Tishbite (1 Kings 17:1); Micaiah, son of Imlah (1 Kings 22:8); Ahijah the Shilonite (1 Kings 11:29); Nathan (2 Sam. 7:2); an unnamed man of God (1 Kings 13:1); and Daniel.[2] There are a number of prophets whose only stated function seemed to be that of historian or court recorder (for example, Shemaiah and Iddo, 2 Chron. 12:15; another Iddo, 2 Chron. 13:22; compare Isaiah, 2 Chron. 26:22).

The prophetic function was not limited to men. The Old Testament mentions prophetesses Miriam (Ex. 15:20); Deborah (Judg. 4:4); the wife of Isaiah (Isa. 8:3); and Huldah (2 Kings 22:14). However, it does not describe their call experiences.

Though nothing is known about the calls of these men and women, the word of God surely came to them in a real and convincing way. It was like fire shut up in their bones which they could not keep to themselves (compare Jer. 20:9).

Each Call Was Different

A comparative study of the calls of the prophets reveals that no two call experiences were exactly alike. The Lord called people both young and old—Jeremiah was probably about twenty, and Moses was eighty. He called rich and poor—Isaiah may have been a member of the royal family; Amos was a sheepherder. He also called the well-educated and the poorly educated—Moses was trained in the wisdom of Egypt; Elisha was a farmer. God called them at different times—Samuel in the dead of night and Elisha while plowing. He met them in unexpected places— Isaiah in the Temple and Ezekiel by a canal in Babylon. He appeared in different ways—to Moses in a burning bush and to Ezekiel in a storm cloud. No specific pattern can be discovered that would characterize all the calls. This diversity serves to remind us that God's sovereignty does not limit him to any one mode of action. In fact, he might be described as the God of surprises.

The Call Was Initiated by God

However, in spite of the diversity and the uniqueness of each call, there are some significant factors common to all of them; and these should be examined.

First, it is clear that the initiative was always with God. God sought out the person and called him. There is never the slightest suggestion that any of the prophets sat down one day and deliberately considered what occupation or profession he would choose to follow. Not one, by careful consideration of his qualifications, the work conditions, the salary scale, and the retirement benefits, concluded that he would become a prophet of God!

Quite the reverse was true. The calls seem to have been so unexpected that several of the prophets argued with God before accepting the responsibility. As a young man Moses may have had some strong stirrings in his heart to be a deliverer of his people. He witnessed the oppression and suffering of his people. One day in a spontaneous outburst of rage, he killed an Egyptian who was mistreating a Hebrew (Ex. 2:11-12; compare Acts 7:25). Forty years passed after his being forced to flee from Egypt to save his life from the wrath of Pharaoh (Ex. 2:15).

Now he was eighty years of age, and those earlier impressions of concern for his people had surely been all but forgotten. Then one day, while taking care of the sheep of his father-in-law, he heard the voice of God calling to him from a burning bush (Ex. 3:1-4).[3]

Isaiah was not seeking or expecting a call from God when he went into the Temple. He was most likely a troubled young man that day. King Uzziah, who had ruled Judah for so many years, had recently died. His death brought a feeling of uncertainty and foreboding throughout the nation. Uzziah's reign had been characterized by stability, prosperity, and devotion to God. There had been no serious threats from outside powers, such as Assyria, during most of his reign. But now what lay in the future? What kind of king would the new ruler be? Would he be weak or strong, devoted to God or wicked? Would he be able to cope with the developing threat from Assyria? These and other questions must have surged through the mind of the uneasy young man as he went into the Temple that day. Perhaps he hoped to find some inner peace and assurance just from being in the presence of God. He was not prepared to encounter God sitting on a throne, "high and lifted up" (Isa. 6:1). Nor did he expect to hear God ask, "Whom shall I send, and who will go for us?" (Isa. 6:8).

Though the circumstances surrounding Jeremiah's call are not given, it is clear that he was not expecting to be called as a prophet. In fact, he vigorously protested that he was too young and inexperienced to be a prophet for God (Jer. 1:6). As a member of a priestly family (1:1), he probably intended to carry on the profession of his family, who had been priests for generations.

Ezekiel was another prophet who was not expecting to be called. It was a critical time in the history of Judah when young Ezekiel went out one day to sit down by the Chebar canal. In a secluded spot he meditated upon recent events and tried to understand what was happening. There were ominous forebodings of calamity at the hands of imperialist Babylonia. Along with King Jehoiachin and other members of the royal court, with craftsmen and skilled workers who could be useful to King Nebuchadnezzar, Ezekiel had been carried into exile in 597 BC. This deportation occurred only about ten years before Jerusalem and its Temple were destroyed by the Babylonians. However, the handwriting was on the wall. Some of the more discerning people were already beginning to ask profound and disturbing theological questions. Was their God really the all-sovereign Creator God of the universe they had believed him to be? Was he about to be defeated by the more powerful Babylonian deities?

In the ancient world of Ezekiel, wars and battles were not considered to be tests of superiority of one general over another or one army over another. Such contests were believed to be in reality struggles between the gods of the opposing armies. The army that emerged victorious proved that its gods had defeated the opposing gods. As proof that the enemy's gods had been overpowered, the captured idols were frequently placed on carts at the head of a procession. They were then led through the streets of the city of the victorious king amidst the shouts of his jubilant people.

Ezekiel may have shared his countrymen's growing pessimism the day he went out to meditate on recent events. However, he was not able to accept the belief that his God was being defeated. He may have briefly entertained another belief that had its adherents in Judah, one which would have been just as devastating to morale. This was the conviction that God in his wrath had turned his back upon his people and would no longer bless them or communicate with them.

Many things may have been troubling his thoughts that day when the sensitive young priest sat down on the banks of the Chebar. However, he was obviously not seeking an appointment as God's prophet. When the Lord appeared to him in the midst of an awesome storm cloud, he was so terrified that he fell on his face. He dared not look up until God ordered him to stand on his feet so that he could speak to him.

The prophet Amos did not describe the events surrounding his call as fully as Moses, Isaiah, Jeremiah, or Ezekiel did. However, in an acrid exchange with the priest Amaziah, he briefly referred to his call. Amaziah had accused Amos of preaching for pay (Amos 7:12). Amos angrily denied that he had become a prophet in order to make his living. He said that he was about his business of shepherding his flocks when God came to him and ordered him to go prophesy to Israel (Amos 7:15). He insisted, "I am not a prophet, nor am I the son of a prophet" (7:14, NASB).

These examples of the calls of several prophets verify that the Old Testament prophets did not choose their vocation. That was a decision which belonged to God. It follows, therefore, that today there is nothing a person can do to be "called by God." There are no buttons to push, no computers to program, and no plan of education or preparation that will ensure a call from God. However, the Christian who wants to know the will of God for his life will more likely discover it by a spirit of willingness than by a rebellious or indifferent attitude.

Tension Was Created by the Call

The second common factor that may be observed in the calls of the prophets is the tension that was created by the call. It was a tension characterized by the prophet's personal struggle to come to terms with his call. He was free to reject the call, but at the same time he felt compelled to accept it. It is true that God was sovereign over the calls, as no one could control or manipulate him. It is equally true that the prophet had the freedom to accept or to reject the call. But when he considered rejecting or renouncing his call, he always felt the divine compulsion that there was nothing else he could do and remain at peace with himself. This freedom to accept or reject the call, coupled with the divine compulsion, sometimes created an almost unbearable tension for a prophet.

Moses, Jeremiah, and Jonah are the prophets who reveal most candidly their struggle with the call. In rapid succession Moses offered four excuses for not accepting his call (Ex. 3:11 to 4:13). It would seem that anyone granted such a spectacular show of God's power at a burning bush would have no reluctance about accepting God's call. How many people have said, "If I could only have tangible evidence of what God wants me to do, then I would do it without a moment's hesitation"? Or, "If God would only give me a sign!" The lesson to be learned from Moses is that, even with such proofs, lingering doubts may remain.

Moses' first excuse seemed reasonable enough. He protested that he was not qualified for the staggering task of freeing his kinsmen from the bondage imposed on them by the greatest world power of that time (Ex. 3:11). After all, he was eighty years of age (Acts 7:23,30). God took care of that excuse by assuring Moses that he would be with him (Ex. 3:12). Moses then offered a second excuse: The people would want to know the name of the God who sent him (3:13). God responded by revealing his personal name, "I AM"⁴ (3:14).

Then Moses raised another very reasonable objection. The people would not believe that the Lord had really appeared to him (4:1). Again God responded by giving Moses a series of miraculous signs that should convince even the most skeptical (4:2-9).

Then the reluctant prophet offered his fourth excuse: He was not an eloquent speaker (4:10). (However, he seemed to have no difficulty voicing his excuses before God!) God recognized the validity of each of the excuses, for each time he offered to provide what Moses lacked. He assured him that he would give the words needed (4:12). With all his excuses demolished, and stripped of all pretense, Moses then pleaded with the Lord to send someone else (4:13)!

The entire dialogue demonstrates that Moses was free to accept or reject his call. However, once he came to terms with the call, he never again showed any reluctance to carry out the tasks assigned to him.[5]

Unlike Moses, though, Jeremiah experienced an ongoing struggle to carry out the will of God. He was reluctant to accept God's call at the outset (Jer. 1:6), using his youth and lack of experience as excuses. He was not like Moses, who never again questioned his call after having his excuses answered. Jeremiah continued to have serious reservations about being God's prophet for some years. In a series of most revealing, intimate glimpses into the heart of the prophet without parallel in the rest of the Bible, Jeremiah confessed his unceasing tension. It was a tension created by his freedom to give up the task assigned him and the divine compulsion to continue it. These intimate glimpses, frequently called the "confessions of Jeremiah," are found in Jer. 11:18-23; 12:1-6; 15:10-21; 17:12-18; 18:18-23; 20:7-18. They reveal the very human reaction of a man who was trying to do God's will, only to discover that the reward for such loyalty was persecution, rejection, physical abuse, and even threats against his life.

In every one of his "confessions," Jeremiah demanded that God bring vengeance on those who were mistreating him. During one moment of despondency, he accused God of being as deceitful and unreliable as a mountain stream. He was thinking of the streams that overflow with water from melting snows in the early spring when it is not especially needed. But those same streams are completely dry in the hot summer when needed most (Jer. 15:18). It was like saying that God fails us when we need him most! On another occasion Jeremiah accused God of "deceiving" him (20:7). The word he actually used is the same word that describes a young man seducing a girl (compare Ex. 22:16).

He also reminded God that he had been faithful in proclaiming God's messages. But how had his diligence been rewarded?

He informed God that he had become a laughingstock to all his friends. His enemies were denouncing him. Even his trusted friends were waiting for his downfall. At that low ebb of alienation from God, he decided that he would renounce his call. He determined to refuse to deliver the oracles given him. After all, no one wanted to hear those messages of "violence and destruction" (Jer. 20:8). No one paid any attention to them, and he had received no thanks or appreciation for his efforts to warn the people.

But just when he resolved that he would never again utter a message given him by God, he experienced the divine compulsion to continue. He described it as fire burning in his bones that could not be contained (20:9). Apparently during this personal crisis Jeremiah resolved once and for all the tension that had characterized his earlier ministry. No further complaints are recorded. Even when imprisoned by the king (32:2) and later lowered into a cistern to die (38:6), he did not complain to God about the unjust treatment accorded him. Never during his darkest moments when he considered abandoning his ministry did he question the genuineness of his call experience.

Moses and Jeremiah both experienced the tension between freedom to accept or to reject the call of God. However, Jonah is probably the prophet who first comes to mind when we think of a reluctant prophet. When God called him to go to Nineveh to deliver a message of judgment against the Ninevites, he took the next boat in the opposite direction. He wanted to get as far away from Nineveh as possible and also to get away from God. In the midst of a great storm at sea, he realized that it was not so easy to avoid being God's prophet. However, in his rebellious state he seemed to prefer being a meal for a fish rather than submit; he asked the sailors to throw him overboard!

Though he finally did go to Nineveh and deliver the message, it is an open question whether he ever did reconcile himself to being God's prophet. We are never told if Jonah changed his attitude toward the Ninevites. The book ends with God asking

Jonah if he is not justified in having compassion on Nineveh. Jonah's reply is not recorded, so it is possible that he never did resolve the tension between the freedom and compulsion experienced in his call.

It is significant that the book ends with a question.[6] It forces the reader to apply the unanswered question to himself: Do we really care enough about lost people to take God's message of forgiveness to them?[7]

If Amos experienced inner conflict in submitting to God's call, he did not tell us. However, he did on several occasions describe his compulsion to speak. In a masterful message that demonstrated the logical relationship between cause and effect (Amos 3:3-8), Amos demonstrated that certain actions will produce anticipated results. He concluded by saying, "A lion has roared! Who will not fear? The Lord GOD has spoken! Who can but prophesy?" (3:8, NASB). This message may have been delivered in response to the Israelites who questioned his right to come to Israel from Judah to preach to them. When Amaziah accused him of preaching for pay, Amos insisted that divine compulsion, not money, was responsible for his ministry. He said, "The LORD took me from following the flock and the LORD said to me, 'Go prophesy to My people Israel'" (7:15, NASB).

The calls from God were not always greeted by reluctance and excuses. Several prophets showed no hesitation in responding to the divine call. God did not directly engage Isaiah to become his prophet. He seemed to be searching for a volunteer when he asked, "Whom shall I send, and who will go for us?" (6:8). Isaiah's eager response suggests that his chief concern was that God might overlook him and call someone else: "Here am I; send me!" It is as though he eagerly waved his hands to get God's attention and pleaded, "Look my way! Let me go for you!"

Ezekiel was another prophet who seemed to have no difficulty responding to the divine imperative. He was willing to accept any task God assigned him. His unquestioning obedience to carry out the most difficult commands set him apart as perhaps the most perfectly self-disciplined of the prophets. On one occasion God ordered him to cut off his hair (5:1-17). To do so would make him an object of ridicule and humiliation, but he did not hesitate. When God ordered him to show no grief when his wife died (24:15-18), his self-mastery enabled him to obey God unquestioningly. Only on one occasion did he show some reluctance to carry out the instructions given to him. That one exception was his unwillingness to break the laws of personal cleanness by preparing his food over human dung (Ezek. 4:9-14; see Lev. 5:3; 7:21)!

Samuel was another prophet who responded on the spot to God's call. When the young child finally understood that it was God calling him in the middle of the night and not the aged priest Eli, he answered the Lord, "Speak, for Thy servant is listening" (1 Sam. 3:10, NASB). His prompt obedience, however, can be attributed to the unquestioning trust of a child rather than denial of self that results from intense personal struggle.

When confronted with the Lord's call most of us are more like Moses, Jeremiah, or Jonah than like Isaiah, Ezekiel, or Samuel. When God calls, he wants commitment that is freely given. When the response is not immediately forthcoming, he deals patiently and graciously with our excuses, as he did with Moses. It is not to our credit that we frequently respond so reluctantly to God's call. However, it is to the praise of God that he waits patiently for us to come around to his will for our lives.

The Individuality of the Prophet Was Preserved

It has already been observed that no two calls of the prophets were alike. The implication of this observation is that God dealt with each prophet as an individual. He never destroyed a prophet's individuality or emasculated his unique personhood.

No prophet became a carbon copy of another—speaking, thinking, and acting with monotonous sameness—simply because he accepted God's call. No two people were more unalike than Jeremiah and Ezekiel. They were contemporaries who preached to the same people at the same period in history. They had the same concern for warning of impending judgment, but their individualism was never in jeopardy. Jeremiah for a time was vacillating, petulant, and complaining. Sometimes the charges he leveled at God were almost blasphemous.

On the other hand, the amazingly self-disciplined prophet Ezekiel unflinchingly stood his ground in the face of a desert storm. A less courageous person might have fled to seek shelter. But because he did not flee, he was granted one of the most remarkable visions of God found anywhere in the Scriptures (Ezek. 1). He was required by God to perform some symbolic acts that would have tried the soul of a lesser person (for example, Ezek. 4:4-8; 5:1-2). His flintlike self-control characterized his entire ministry.

Though they all were preaching God's message, each prophet had his own style that reflected his individuality. A careful reading of the prophets readily reveals their stylistic differences. Isaiah reached heights of poetic grandeur in his proclamation of God's word, whereas the messages of Haggai and Malachi were prosaic and plain. Differences in style of delivery can readily be observed in today's preachers also.

These observations concerning the prophets suggest that when a person is called by God, he should not expect to become so completely different that even his best friend would not recognize him! A rather unimaginative, unemotional person will probably deliver God's messages in a rather unimaginative, unemotional manner. An extremely sensitive, creative person may proclaim God's messages with eloquence and style. A person whose vocabulary was somewhat limited before being called will not likely find his mouth suddenly filled with words that even he does not understand!

These observations do not imply that a person will hamper the word of God by his personal limitations. Nor does it mean that because of his many talents another will embellish it beyond what God really intended to communicate. Rather, they remind us that God has in both cases chosen the vessel through whom the message will be communicated. If it is God's message, it will accomplish its intended purpose regardless of the vessel through which the message is communicated (Isa. 55:11).

It is true that one's individuality is not obliterated by a divine call, but it is equally true that the called person will never be the same again. The imprint of the hand of God on a life is indelible. The call separates him from the past and from his own priorities. It thrusts him into new situations and sometimes into new surroundings. Moses found himself taken from a rugged desert wilderness to the court of Pharaoh. Amos found himself taken from the quiet pastoral life with his flocks to the cities of Israel. There he was required to denounce the people for their oppression, immorality, and debauchery, and to warn them of the impending day of judgment. A reluctant Jonah found himself walking the streets of far-off Nineveh.

Even the person who rejects the call of God in the exercise of his freedom of choice will never be the same again. He will not be able to erase the memory of a divine encounter. His rejection of God's call will be like a scar cut deeply across his heart. It will never be forgotten completely. Though God may find some other way to use him, he will always remember that he was called but did not respond. He will not forget that God communicated his love and his divine will through the call.

The greatest honor that can come to anyone is to have God entrust his word to that person to proclaim to others. It is far better to accept the call with whatever personal sacrifice it entails than to live with the memory that we rejected God's call. However reasonable our excuses may seem to us, they reveal our unwillingness to trust God with our day-by-day existence. We may be willing to trust eternity to him; but when we are unwilling to accept his call, we are saying that we do not trust him with this life. Nor do we have confidence in his ability to make this life the best and most fulfilling kind of life. What we really believe is that our plans are better than what he proposes or that he does not have our best interests at heart.

While I was a seminary student and serving as pastor of a small church, a member of the church came one day with tears streaming down her cheeks. Her story was one that has been repeated many times. God had called her as a teenager to the mission field. She pushed the call into the background because she was afraid she would have to abandon her own dreams and give up some "good times."

The years passed. She married and raised her children. She and her husband were model Christians in the community and leaders in the church. Her life had served as an inspiration to many young people. Now middle-aged and in poor health, she could no longer go to the mission field even if she desired.

God had given her a second-best plan to fulfill and was using her. But she could never forget that years earlier God had called and she had said no. Her parting words that afternoon were, "Whenever you have an opportunity, plead with young people not to make the mistake I made."

If only we can believe that the will of God is "good, pleasing and perfect" (Rom. 12:2, NIV), how much more likely will we be to accept his call.

The Purpose of the Call

One other aspect of the call which should be considered is its purpose. Aside from the obvious necessity of letting a prophet know what God wanted him to do, what practical purposes did the call serve? Wasn't it quite obvious to Moses that the Israelites needed to be delivered from Egyptian bondage? Did God have to resort to a rather dramatic device of speaking from a burning bush before Moses could have acted on behalf of his people? Wasn't it obvious to men like Jeremiah and Ezekiel that their nation had become so morally and politically corrupt that it could not survive? Did they need a "call" in order to know that they should warn their people that the course they were pursuing could only lead to calamity?

Did Hosea have to undergo the bitter experience of a wife who deserted her husband and children before he could tell the Israelites that God loved them and wanted to forgive them? Did God have to wake the child Samuel out of his sleep in the middle of the night to "call" him? Didn't Jonah know that God was so compassionate and longsuffering that he wanted even the Ninevites to know about his love? Was it necessary to scare him half out of his wits by a storm and a few nights in a fish's stomach before he could know that he should share his God with the Ninevites? In Jonah's case, the answer is an unqualified yes. He did know what kind of God he was dealing with but just didn't want the Ninevites to know his God (Jonah 4:2).

Unless there were some purpose for a "call" other than informing a person of a need, couldn't any committed man or woman of God decide where to go and what to do? Isn't it only a matter of determining one's talents and the needs one is best suited to handle? Human logic says "Yes, of course," but divine logic says, "Wait for the call of God."

Unfortunately, there is a popular concept of a call that is much too restrictive. The calls of God are much broader than a few traditional categories such as preacher, missionary, or paid staff worker. In broadest terms the call of God is the experience through which God tells a Christian what he wants him to do with his life.

If one is willing to equate the call of God with the revelation of God's plan for his life, there are two inescapable conclusions that follow. First, it means that God calls every Christian. Or, expressed another way, God has a plan for each of us and wants us to know what plan he has for our lives. It is not logical or in keeping with God's nature to say to a few Christians, "I have a plan for your life, and I will tell you what it is." But to the others he would say, "I don't really care what you do with your life; make your own plans." Therefore, every Christian ought to have the same assurance of a call as does a pastor or a missionary,* whether doctor, lawyer, merchant, farmer, or housewife. Divine revelation in the realm of vocational guidance is not only desirable; it is attainable.

There is a second conclusion to be drawn from this concept of the call. Since God created us and gave us our natural abilities and talents, he knows what we are best suited to do. Therefore, if we follow his plan for our lives, we will be happier than if we follow our own plans. It is a well-known fact that people who find the most enjoyment in their work have a natural ability or interest in that work. The person who is unhappy in a job is usually not suited for it. A person who cannot carry a tune would not likely be too happy performing the lead role in *Aida!*

There are Christians who go for years without ever discovering that God really wants us to be happy and that he knows how we can best achieve happiness. There is a mistaken belief that one is doing the will of God only if he is absolutely miserable. Quite the reverse is true. One only achieves genuine happiness by doing the will of God.

Returning, then, to the affirmation that the call has a purpose, what are the purposes of a call? For the Old Testament prophets, there were three significant reasons for their calls.

The Call Determined the Emphasis of Ministry

First, the call determined the direction and emphasis of the ministry of the prophet. In other words, something transpired in that initial call experience that forever stamped the unique ministry of the prophet. In Isaiah's call, he saw God high and lifted up and heard the seraphim say, "Holy, holy, holy." The scene imprinted itself so indelibly upon him that throughout his ministry he returned again and again to the theme of the transcendence and holiness of God. No other prophet emphasized these two attributes of God quite so much as did Isaiah.

In his call at the burning bush, Moses was given one commission. That was to deliver Israel from bondage and to lead the people to the Promised Land. The next forty years of his life were obsessed with carrying out this one task. There were probably very few waking hours during those years when he was not thinking about getting the people to the Promised Land. He understood that the only way to reach their destination was through absolute obedience to God; therefore, the singular appeal of his messages to Israel was to obey God. Where did Moses learn that God required obedience? It was at the time of his call. God rejected all his excuses (Ex. 3:11 to 4:17). He made it quite clear that an eighty-year-old man who would obey God unreservedly could do mighty deeds. Also, Moses probably never forgot that his continued resistance to God's call caused him to lose the privilege of being God's spokesman to the Israelites. God gave that honor to Aaron (Ex. 4:13-16).

The call of Hosea was indissolubly linked with his personal marital tragedy. Through it he learned the extent of God's love and his desire to forgive Israel and restore her to himself. No other prophet in the Old Testament delivered the message of love and forgiveness quite as effectively as Hosea. For this reason he has been called the apostle John of the Old Testament.

From these biblical examples it can be seen that a careful examination of one's call will usually reveal that the general thrust and emphasis of one's vocation has been largely determined by that call.

Have you ever wondered why one pastor preaches mostly evangelistic messages? Another, messages of social concern? Another, missions? Another, holy living? If you could know the circumstances of his call, you would understand why his ministry is characterized by one special concern above all others.

The Call Authenticated the Prophet's Message

A second and essential purpose of the call was to authenticate the message and ministry of the prophet before those who heard him. Moses doubted that the people would believe him if he went to them to tell them that he had a divine commission to free them from Egyptian bondage. However, when he did return to Egypt and assembled the people, he had Aaron repeat to them all that had happened in the desert. The result was that "the people believed" (Ex. 4:31). There would be many times later when the people would not believe Moses, but on this crucial occasion they did believe. Moses' conviction that he had truly been called by God to be their deliverer must have communicated itself to the downtrodden Israelites.

The Scripture record does not tell how many years elapsed after the child Samuel was called before he began exercising his prophetic ministry. However, we are told that "All Israel from Dan even to Beersheba knew that Samuel was confirmed as a prophet of the LORD" (1 Sam. 3:20, NASB). The call authenticated his prophetic status in the eyes of the people.

Even though the Israelites might know the prophet's message was from God, it did not follow that they would obey. In fact, God told Isaiah when he called him that the people would not understand and that their ears would be dull and their eyes dim (Isa. 6:9-10). He told Jeremiah not to be dismayed by the people's unresponsiveness and warned him that they would fight against him (Jer. 1:17-19). He told Ezekiel that the people were stubborn and rebellious and that he would be like one sitting on scorpions (Ezek. 2:3-6). But in every case, whether they listened or not, they would know that a prophet had been among them (2:5). Ezekiel did enjoy a brief period of popularity with the people. His acclaim did not come about because they were willing to obey God. Instead it was because Ezekiel's words entertained them "like a sensual song by one who has a beautiful voice and plays well on an instrument" (33:32, NASB).

Though the weak and vacillating King Zedekiah finally refused to follow the advice Jeremiah gave him during the siege of Jerusalem, he considered it. He wanted to follow Jeremiah's counsel, which he recognized as being from God. But he was also anxious to please his courtiers, whom he feared might kill him if he listened to the prophet (Jer. 38:14-28). Unfortunately for both the king and Jerusalem, the hapless Zedekiah chose to ignore the advice of Jeremiah, though he knew it was an authentic message from God. His refusal to submit to the Babylonians sealed the doom of Jerusalem.

A note of authority marked the words of all these prophets, and their audiences could not ignore it. They knew that a prophet had been among them, whether they obeyed his words or not. Likewise, there is a degree of skill and proficiency that characterizes every person who is doing God's will that others will notice, whatever his profession may be.

The Call Enabled a Prophet to Stay with the Task

A final, necessary purpose for a call was to enable the prophet to keep going in the midst of trying circumstances that might tempt him to abandon his task. One wonders if Moses would have had the inner fortitude to continue traveling through the wilderness for forty years with a rebellious, complaining people if he had not experienced the call of God. In fact, on several occasions, a wrathful God offered to destroy the disobedient Israelites and raise up a great nation of Moses. To his credit the man of God resisted the very tempting offer in favor of completing the task for which he had been called (Ex. 32:10; Num. 14:12).

More than any other prophet, Jeremiah exemplifies the man who stayed with the task because the call could not be blotted out. On several occasions he was on the verge of renouncing his ministry (Jer. 15:15-18; 20:7-9); but try as he would, he was unable to put the call of God out of his mind. The message was like fire burning in his bones. Though he sometimes complained about his mistreatment for doing God's will, he never did question whether God had actually called him. And that indelibly abiding conviction that God had called was all that kept him committed to the task.

Some mission boards today query prospective candidates, especially at the point of a call. If not convinced that the candidate has experienced a genuine call to the mission field, they will not appoint him. In fact, some boards require the same evidence of a call on the part of one spouse that they require of the other. This requirement was established long before the equal rights movement was launched! A "Ruth commitment" of "where you go I will go" will not suffice.

Experience has taught foreign mission boards that if either husband or wife does not have a deep sense of call, the resignation ratio is much higher. When the going becomes difficult on the foreign field (and it usually does), it is very easy to throw in the towel. The missionary could rationalize, "God didn't really call me here in the first place, so I'll return home where life is easier." How many ministers have been tempted to sit down and write their memoirs, "Why I Left the Ministry"—only to be reminded of the divine commission that cannot be so easily abandoned!

What has been said about minister and missionary also holds true for the lay person. He will encounter disappointments and frustrations in whatever vocation to which God has called him. A conviction that "this is what God wants me to do" will keep him going when otherwise he might be tempted to turn in his resignation.

Conclusion

The calls of the prophets in the Old Testament were complex. They were suited to the needs and personality of the individual prophet. They did not destroy his sense of individuality, but they did forever afterward set him apart and mark him as a distinctive servant of the Lord.

The call served many practical purposes. For the prophet it was the most authentic and unforgettable experience of his life. He would not have explained it as psychologically self-induced or as a kind of therapeutic dialogue with himself. If it had been no more than a psychological booster shot, it is unlikely that it would have carried the prophets through the trying times they frequently experienced. Many prophets were put to death for claiming to speak in the name of the Lord (Jer. 2:30); but there is no evidence that any of them, when confronting martyrdom, renounced his call.

The call, then, was decisive in the prophetic experience. It was the door that opened the way for the prophetic ministry. Its recollection impelled the prophet to continue proclaiming "Thus says the Lord" in the face of overwhelming adversity.

Notes

1. Though Abraham is not usually thought of as a prophet, he is called one in Genesis 20:7.

2. In the Hebrew Bible the book of Daniel is not included with the Prophets but is found in a section called the Ketubim ("Writings"), along with books such as Psalms, Proverbs, Esther, and Ruth.

3. The use of the participle requiring a translation "the bush *was burning*" (3:2) has caused someone to comment, "The bush did not burn up; it did not burn down. It just burned."

4. The meaning of this name has occupied the attention of Bible students for centuries. It identifies God as the covenant God of Israel. In the third-person form in which it usually appears (rather than the first person as in 3:14) it is spelled YHWH or JHVH. It appears without vowels because the Hebrew language was for centuries written without vowels. The pronunciation of words was transmitted orally from one generation to the next, so even without written vowels the people knew how to pronounce the words. However, with the passing of time this particular name of God became so sacred that the Hebrew people would not speak it. Therefore, the pronunciation was eventually forgotten, and today no one can be sure how it was actually pronounced. Most linguists believe that with vowels added the name was pronounced Yahweh. It usually is translated in English Bibles as "the Lord" and sometimes as "Jehovah." It comes from the Hebrew word "to be" and is clearly linked to the self-existence of God. It has been interpreted to mean "I am what I am," "I am because I am," "I will be what I will be," or "I will be whatever you need me to be." It has also been interpreted to mean "I cause to be" (that is, "I bring into being" or "I am the one who creates"). The name YHWH is referred to frequently as the sacred tetragrammaton (from a Greek word that means "four letters").

5. With one exception—when Moses became angry and disobeyed God's instructions (Num. 20:1-13). However, even on that occasion Moses was not deliberately refusing to obey God's orders. He was so angry with the complaining Israelites that he vented his feelings by striking the rock instead of speaking to it, as God had commanded him.

6. Only one other book in the Bible, Nahum, ends with a question. Nahum, like Jonah, directed his messages to Nineveh.

7. James Hardee Kennedy, *Studies in the Book of Jonah* (Nashville: Broadman Press, 1956), p. 87, phrases the central issue of Jonah succinctly: "The Supreme Issue: Gourds or Souls." The statement is too incisive for comfort. Do we really care about lost people more than our pursuit of material possessions? Do we devote the same energy to winning the lost that we give to the acquisition of creature comforts? We know the right answer to these questions, but our actions frequently belie our words.

8. Frank Stagg, *New Testament Theology* (Nashville: Broadman Press, 1962), p. 253, calls attention to the fact that the word for "clergy" comes from a Greek word, *klēroō*, "to cast lots." Just as the lot was cast that fell on Jonah (Jonah 1:7), and just as the apostle to replace Judas was chosen by casting lots (Acts 1:23-26), so a minister is one who has been chosen by God's process of selection to a life of service. Stagg goes ahead to insist that all Christians are "clergy." He means that the "lot" (klēros) has fallen on them—that is, that they have been set apart by God (see 1 Pet. 2:9).

2

"Thus Says the Lord"
(The Authority of the Prophet)

Because he knew he had been called by God, the Hebrew prophet stood before his people and fearlessly proclaimed his messages. He insisted that his authority for speaking came from God. Therefore, the people should have listened to him. If they had, they would have been spared the judgment that came upon them.

The prophet knew that he was authorized by God to prophesy, but how were the people to know? One might reply, "The answer is easy; the Bible tells us these men were prophets!" However, if we had lived among the people of Judah around 590 BC, would we have identified an old man who walked the dusty streets of Jerusalem day after day for almost forty years as the prophet Jeremiah? With tears streaming down his cheeks, he accosted every passerby who would stop and listen. He warned that Jerusalem was going to be destroyed if the people did not turn back to God. He didn't have a halo, union card, or any other credential that would establish him as a prophet.

In fact, the people heard this eccentric person proclaim the same monotonous message of impending doom for so many years that he became an object of ridicule to them. They mocked him when they met him on the streets and asked in effect, "What burdensome word do you have from the Lord today, old man?" (compare Jer. 23:33). They taunted him to let God's words come on them (17:15), for they did not fear God's wrath. They also scorned Ezekiel by saying, "The days are long and every vision fails" (Ezek. 12:22, NASB). They did not believe Jeremiah or Ezekiel spoke with authority from God; else they would not have ridiculed them.

It is not necessary to say how different Israel's history might have been if she had recognized the authority behind the messages of the prophets. Instead, the people preferred to believe those false prophets (and prophetesses, Ezek. 13:17-19) who said in effect, "Peace, peace! Everything is all right. Don't worry about the threat of impending judgment. After all, doesn't the temple of God stand in our midst as a visible symbol of his continued presence and care for us?" (See Jer. 6:14; Ezek. 13:10.) Israel could not distinguish between false and true prophets, and this failure was her undoing.

Difficulty of Identifying a Prophet

The difficulty of identifying the true prophets of God is not only important in the context of Israel's history. It also has contemporary relevance. How can we know whether a person today who claims to have a message from God is truly a spokesman for God or a fraud? How many times have we read in the newspaper the words of a self-appointed prophet who announces that the end of the world is coming shortly? Or perhaps he preaches that God's judgment is about to fall on the nation. We shrug off such a person as a harmless crank. But what if he really were a latter-day prophet of God with an authoritative word of warning from the Lord? Then we would be well advised to listen to him.

Once just before I stood in the pulpit to preach, I saw a man come in quietly and sit down on the back row. Dressed in old clothes and of unkempt appearance, he obviously was not a member of the church. As sometimes happens to preachers, I assumed that the Lord had brought this derelict of humanity out of a gutter or a rescue mission to hear my preaching! I began to imagine that he would be gloriously saved and transformed before the evening ended. He seemed reasonably attentive throughout the service. The invitation was prolonged as long as one decently could, but there was no response from our visitor. So, a little disappointed, I called on a member to pronounce a closing benediction.

Just as he finished and before the congregation could begin to leave, a strong, clear voice was heard from the back of the room: "Could I have your attention?" All eyes quickly focused on the visitor who had not responded to my invitation. In a firm but polite voice he told us he was a prophet of God. He said that our nation was going to be destroyed in a short time (I have forgotten the date he set). Then he courteously said, "Thank you," and walked out, leaving all of us stunned for a few moments. Then someone laughed a little nervously, and everyone relaxed and forgot the incident. Obviously he wasn't a prophet of God, for the incident took place several years ago. *But suppose he had been?* It was easier to laugh at him than to take him seriously, but it was also easier to laugh at Jeremiah than to take him seriously.

The people of Jerusalem probably shrugged off Jeremiah as a harmless crank, if not an annoying public nuisance. However, when Jerusalem lay in smoldering ruins about them, they must have wailed, "We should have listened to Jeremiah."

Wherein lay the prophet's authority? His authority was not dependent upon his ability as a speaker. In the Old Testament one fact alone determined his authority: Had he been called and commissioned by God? If·so, he was a true prophet; if not, he was a false prophet.

There is no single word in the Hebrew language meaning "false prophet" that would correspond to the Greek word in the New Testament, *pseudoprophētēs.*[1] However, the idea is clearly expressed in phrases such as "lying spirit" (1 Kings 22:23), "lying words" (Jer. 7:4), "divining lies" (Ezek. 22:28), "daubed . . . whitewash" (Ezek. 22:28), "false vision" (Jer. 14:14), "prophets shall become wind" (Jer. 5:13).

Sincerity Was Not Sufficient

Sincerity cannot be considered a distinguishing mark of a true prophet, for many false prophets were sincere, though self-deceived. Not all the false prophets deliberately deluded the people, though, of course, many did. When Hananiah announced a message that was contrary to what Jeremiah had been preaching, he was convinced that he was speaking in the name of the Lord. Even Jeremiah did not immediately challenge Hananiah. He went away to receive assurance from the Lord. Only then did he return to denounce Hananiah for making the people trust in a lie (Jer. 28:1-17).

Being Called "Prophet" Was Not Sufficient

Calling a man a prophet did not necessarily mean he was one. The biblical writers did not distinguish the false prophet from the true prophet by calling him by some title other than "prophet." "Prophet" is used to describe the 450 representatives of Baal and the 400 spokesmen of Asherah (1 Kings 18:19). Jeremiah 28:1 speaks of "Hananiah . . . the prophet." It is only by reading the account that follows that we know Hananiah was a false prophet.

Saying "Thus Says the Lord" Was Not Sufficient

Prefacing a message with "Thus says the Lord" did not necessarily prove a man was a true prophet, for the false prophets introduced their messages with the same words (Jer. 28:2; Ezek. 13:2,6-7). This phrase had an interesting usage in the ancient world. In the ancient Near East kings frequently sent messengers or heralds to various parts of the kingdom to read royal decrees to their subjects. If the messenger announced to the assembled crowd that the decree was his own, he would have been ignored or dealt with more severely. However, when they heard him announce, "Thus says the king of Assyria" or "Thus says the King of Babylon" (compare 2 Chron. 18:26; 32:10;

2 Kings 18:19), we can be sure the people listened in respectful silence, for the phrase carried the authority of the king and his army behind it. The subjects knew they had no choice but to obey.

The prophets borrowed this "messenger formula" (as it is called by Old Testament scholars) and revised it to introduce their messages with "Thus says the Lord." Their audiences understood that they were claiming the authority of their ruler, God himself, for what they were about to say. Not only did the prophets usually begin their messages with this phrase; they interrupted their messages frequently with the same reminder. For example, of the eight verses in Zechariah 8:2-9, six begin with "Thus says the Lord."

However, as already noted, there was no absolute proof that a man was a true prophet simply because he introduced his oracle with "Thus says the Lord." The false prophets did not hesitate to use the same solemn words (Jer. 28:1-2; Ezek. 13:6-7), though their messages came from their own minds (Ezek. 13:17).

Criteria for Identifying a True Prophet

Ability as a speaker, sincerity, title, or claim of authority from God cannot be depended upon to distinguish a false prophet from a true one. What criteria, then, can be applied to the Old Testament prophets to determine whether they were true or false prophets? The answer is not easy to find, but the following ten criteria may help us know if we are hearing a spokesman sent from God.

The Words of the Prophet Came True

There are only two clearly established Old Testament criteria for distinguishing true from false prophets. Both are found in the book of Deuteronomy. The first is the test of fulfillment, found in Deuteronomy 18:22: "When a prophet speaks in the name of the LORD, if the thing does not come about or come true, that is the thing which the LORD has not spoken. The prophet has spoken it presumptuously; you shall not be afraid of him" (NASB).

If the words of the prophet came true, he was recognized as a true prophet. After the warnings of the destruction of Jerusalem given by Jeremiah and Ezekiel came true, the people flocked around them to acknowledge that they were prophets of God because they had satisfied the Deuteronomic test of fulfillment (Jer. 42:1-6; Ezek. 33:30-33).

It would seem that no other criterion was necessary since the fulfillment test would be so easy to establish. However, this test is not so foolproof as it may appear at first glance. There frequently was a long lapse of time between proclamation and fulfillment. When fulfillment did occur, it was sometimes too late to benefit by knowing that the man truly was a prophet.

Jeremiah preached for forty years that Jerusalem was going to be destroyed. After thirty-nine years of hearing such dire predictions, the people were convinced that Jeremiah was a false prophet because nothing he said had come true. In fact, they ridiculed him publicly and privately. Unfortunately, when the fulfillment occurred—the destruction of Jerusalem—it was too late to profit from the knowledge that Jeremiah had been telling the truth.

Micah may have been branded a false prophet for a considerable time. He correctly announced that "Zion shall be plowed as a field;/Jerusalem shall become a heap of ruins,/and the mountain of the house a wooded height" (Mic. 3:12, RSV). But his warnings were issued more than a century before they came true. In fact, when Jeremiah voiced a similar warning against Jerusalem, the people were so angry that he would utter such blasphemous words that they were ready to mob him on the spot. Fortunately for Jeremiah, someone recalled that Micah had uttered similar words a hundred years earlier. King Hezekiah believed him and did not put him to death (Jer. 26:16-19). Consequently, they decided not to kill Jeremiah. In effect, Micah stepped out of the past to save Jeremiah's life.

1 Kings 13 tells of a nameless man of God from Judah who came to Jeroboam I at Bethel and foretold the destruction of the altar upon which Jeroboam was about to offer sacrifice. However, the altar was not actually destroyed until three hundred years later (2 Kings 23:15-16).

Joel also could have suffered the stigma of "false prophet" in his lifetime if the fulfillment test had been applied to him. Joel predicted an outpouring of the Spirit of God accompanied by cosmic upheavals (Joel 2:28-32). It was hundreds of years later on the day of Pentecost that the apostle Peter announced that Joel's prophecy had been fulfilled. He interpreted the strange behavior that accompanied the filling of the believers with the Spirit of God as fulfillment of Joel's prophecy (Acts 2:14-21). In the intervening centuries many probably concluded that Joel was a false prophet.

The conditional aspect of some prophecies could invalidate their fulfillment (for example, Jer. 18:7-10; Deut. 28:1). When the prophecy begins with "if," it is relatively easy to identify it as a conditional prophecy. But what about those prophecies that contain implied conditions? In Jonah 3:4 there must have been an implied condition, or possibly stated but not recorded. The condition was that if the Ninevites would repent, they would not be destroyed. Why, otherwise, did Jonah hesitate to go preach to Israel's worst enemy? He should have been delighted to announce, "Yet forty days and Nineveh shall be overthrown."

Haggai 2:19 offers another example of an implied condition. Is the promise of prosperity and blessing found there conditional, though not stated? It must have been, for good times did not follow the temple's completion.

Do any of the promises to Israel in the Old Testament contain implied conditions? Or must every unfulfilled promise to Israel yet be fulfilled? Scholars and Bible students are not agreed on the answer to this question.

We conclude, therefore, that the fulfillment test is valid for knowing whether a man was truly a prophet. However, it was a

very difficult test to apply, for when the test was finally vali-
dated, it was usually too late to be of any benefit to those who
had heard the prophetic warning.

He Encouraged Faithfulness to God

The second biblical criterion for the true prophet is found in
the thirteenth chapter of Deuteronomy. In summary, it says that
the true prophet encouraged faithfulness to God. Even if his
prophecies were fulfilled, he was not to be considered a true
prophet if he led the people astray from God or encouraged them
to worship other gods.

The true prophets thoroughly understood one admonition that
had been given them from the time of Moses. That was the
command to have no other gods before the Lord. Moses warned
the Israelites that they should not be enticed by the Canaanite
deities when they entered the land, or they would bring about
their own destruction (Deut. 7:1-5; 11:16-17). He told them that
the Canaanites must be driven out of the land. He knew that
when the Hebrews were introduced to the alluring sexual rituals
the Canaanites practiced in the name of religion, they would not
be able to resist them. Instead of being proselyters, they would
be proselyted; and that is exactly what happened. Even before
they entered the land they encountered the Canaanite deities at
Baal-peor and succumbed to their charms (Num. 25:1-5).

Hosea compared the idolatry of the Israelites to harlotry (Hos.
2:2; compare Ezek. 16:15-17). Jeremiah ridiculed the worship of
idols (Jer. 10:1-16). The book of Isaiah contains more denunciation and ridicule of idolatry than any other book of the Old
Testament (Isa. 40:18-20; 41:5-7; 44:9-20; 46:1-7). Elijah (1
Kings 18) and Hosea (Hos. 14:2-3) also added their words of
warning concerning idolatry, but they were of no avail. Israel
was determined to go after other gods. The people preferred to
listen to the false prophets who encouraged them to turn away
from God (Jer. 18:12).

Idol worship was appealing because it gave the worshiper an

undefined sense of control over his deity. He made the god; he carried it about; and, presumably, if the god did not perform satisfactorily, it could be smashed or thrown into the fire.

The true prophets were characterized by their devotion to the one God and by their insistence that all Israel worship him alone. As a definitive criterion, however, this one was not always helpful, for few false prophets blatantly called on the people to renounce God. Instead, they said, "Worship God *and* Baal." Moreover, their messages often had a show of piety that misled the people. They appealed to "the temple, the temple" to assure the people that all was well.

He Was Called by God

Another mark of the true prophet was the call he had received from God. The concept of the call has been discussed at length in the preceding chapter and therefore does not need to be repeated here.

The call was a mark of the genuine prophet, as no false prophet was called by God. However, it was a difficult test to apply objectively. One prophet could not always recognize another prophet. An unnamed "man of God" delivered a message of judgment to Jeroboam but later was deceived by another man who claimed to be a prophet also (1 Kings 13). Hananiah claimed he had been sent by God. It was only after a time of prayer that Jeremiah was able to return and confront the impostor and say, "The Lord has not sent you" (Jer. 28:15).

The call experience is by its very nature subjective. Only two people can really know if the call is genuine—God and the person called. Some standards may be applied whereby we can reasonably conclude that a person has been called (Matt. 7:20). However, there is always the possibility that we can be fooled, and even the one claiming to be a prophet may deceive himself.

To compound the difficulty of applying the call as a legitimate test of the true prophet, there were occasions when even a called person did not speak God's word. Miriam and Aaron (both called by God) confronted Moses one day and said, "Has the LORD indeed spoken only through Moses? Has he not spoken through us as well?" (Num. 12:2, NASB). The Lord repudiated both of them on the spot (12:4-15) because they were criticizing Moses for having married a Cushite woman (12:1).

Even Moses on one occasion did not speak and act according to God's will. This occurred in the wilderness of Zin when the people demanded water to drink. God instructed Moses to speak to a rock to bring forth water. Instead, Moses struck the rock. Because of this one lapse, God would not allow him to enter the Promised Land with the rest of Israel (Num. 20:1-12).

See also Jer. 15:19-21, where God rebuked Jeremiah for speaking words that were not true. On another occasion Jeremiah did not speak the truth out of fear for his life (38:24-27).

He Was Possessed by God's Word

The prophet identified himself with the word of the Lord and seemed to be possessed by it. Several prophets described the dramatic moment when God's word became a part of them. In Isaiah's call experience his lips were touched with the burning coal in the hand of one of the seraphim (Isa. 6:6-7). This gesture symbolized the necessity of one's cleansing in order to be a spokesman for God.

One of Moses' major objections when he was called was that he would not be able to speak. The Lord responded that he would give him the words to say (Ex. 4:10-12).

Jeremiah offered an excuse similar to that of Moses by insisting he was not able to speak (Jer. 1:6). The Lord responded by touching his mouth and saying, "Behold, I have put my words in your mouth" (1:9). In recalling his initial experience of receiving God's word, Jeremiah said, "Thy words were found and I ate them,/And Thy words became for me a joy and the delight of my heart" (Jer. 15:16, NASB).

In his initial encounter with God Ezekiel also experienced an unusual identification with God's word. God told him to eat a scroll which was written on both sides. He described it as being as sweet as honey in his mouth. From that moment on he was possessed by the compulsion to proclaim God's messages (Ezek. 2:8 to 3:3). For at least seven and one-half years of his ministry, he was so possessed by the word of the Lord that he did not speak a single word unless it was a message from God (3:26-27; 33:22).

We would expect God's words to be spoken only by a servant of the Lord. However, the divine oracle was not always communicated through a man of God. Pharaoh Necho spoke at the Lord's command to King Josiah. Josiah refused to listen to Necho's warning not to fight against the Egyptians, even though Pharaoh's words were "from the mouth of God" (2 Chron. 35:21-22). Balaam tried to curse the Israelites but could only bless them when he opened his mouth (Num. 22—24). It is uncertain whether Balaam should be classed with the prophets of God; but on this occasion, at least, he spoke God's message. God called King Nebuchadnezzar "my servant" (Jer. 25:9). In turn the Babylonian monarch spoke concerning God: "His kingdom is an everlasting kingdom" (Dan. 4:3; see also 4:34-37).

For the prophets there was a dynamic quality in God's word that captivated and compelled them to deliver his messages. They shared the widespread belief in the ancient Near East that a word, once it was spoken, acquired independent existence. Words were believed to be far more than sounds that escaped the mouth only for the purpose of communicating the thoughts of one person to another, afterward evaporating into the atmosphere. They were believed to be an extension of the speaker. Words, especially in the form of blessings and curses, continued to exist until they brought about their stated purpose.

There is a phrase found 123 times in the Old Testament that reveals better than any other this unique belief about words: "The word of the Lord came to . . . ." For example, the word of the Lord came to Isaiah (38:4), to Jeremiah (1:4), to Ezekiel (1:3), and to other prophets (Hos. 1:1; Joel 1:1; Mic. 1:1; Hag. 2:10). The word of the Lord came to men of such different eras and backgrounds as Abraham (Gen. 15:1) and Solomon (1 Kings

6:11). The phrase does not mean that the word came in some tangible form like inscriptions on golden plates dropped down from heaven. Nor should it be understood as a kind of offhand way of saying, "This idea came to me" or "That thought just occurred to me."

The true significance of the phrase cannot begin to be understood until it is examined in the original Hebrew language. The verb translated as "came" in our Bibles is the Hebrew verb "to be." Literally, it should be translated "The word of the Lord was to . . . ." However, that translation sounds unnatural to our ears. It is not the way we speak, so English translations have accommodated themselves to words that sound more natural. However, in the process of accommodation, these translations may lose some of the meaning of the phrase. To translate a verb of being by an action verb may change the essential meaning. When they said, "The word of the Lord came to . . . ," the biblical writers were trying to communicate to us that the word of the Lord had its own existence. The phrase could be translated "The word of the Lord became active reality" or "The word of the Lord came alive."

Only when we grasp the Hebrew belief about words can we begin to understand why the prophets were possessed by the Lord's word. His words were living and powerful. They could accomplish the promise or the threat contained in them. Isaac pronounced a blessing upon Jacob instead of Esau as a result of a disguise assumed by the younger twin. However, he was unable to retract it because he knew that it no longer belonged to him. Though unintentionally, it had been transferred to Jacob (Gen. 27).

Jewish people still exhibit this belief in the self-existence of God's words that were spoken as promises. Whatever one's political sympathies may be in the current Arab-Israeli conflict in the Middle East, the unyielding stubbornness of the Jewish people in holding on to the land cannot be understood apart from understanding their conviction that God promised the land to Abraham and his descendants. The promise is still "alive" for them and transcends all other subsequent title deeds to the land. They appear willing to risk a world holocaust rather than give up land they say is theirs.

We talk about solar power, the power of hydrogen bombs, and the power of neutron bombs. However, if we could compress all known sources of power into one container, they would not begin to approach the power that the prophets believed was contained in the word of the Lord. When Jeremiah hesitated to respond to God's call because of his inability to speak effectively, God assured him that it would not be Jeremiah's power or ability that would accomplish the results. It would be the power of God's word placed in the young prophet's mouth that would "pluck up and . . . break down,/. . . destroy and . . . overthrow,/. . . build and . . . plant" (Jer. 1:10).

Through the prophet Isaiah God said, "My word . . . will not return to me empty, but will accomplish what I desire" (Isa. 55:11, NIV). The New Testament echoes this same conviction. It says that power to accomplish whatever God speaks is inherent in the word of God: "The word of God is living and active. Sharper than any doubled-edged sword . . ." (Heb. 4:12, NIV). Sometimes we become discouraged by world events and what appears to be the inactivity, if not the impotence, of God in the face of evil's rapid spread everywhere. At those times it is good to remind ourselves that what he has spoken will be accomplished. "The Son is . . . sustaining all things by his powerful word" (Heb. 1:3, NIV). The promise that one day "every knee should bow, . . . and every tongue confess that Jesus Christ is Lord, to the glory of God the Father" (Phil. 2:10-11, NIV) will be fulfilled. God still reigns as sovereign and will triumph over all the forces of evil.

The Old Testament also reveals another Israelite belief about the word spoken by God, and that is the creative activity contained in the spoken word. Simply by speaking, God was able to bring the world into being and everything that is in it. Eight times in the brief creation story in Genesis 1 we are told how God created. Each creative act is introduced by "And God said." "And God said, 'Let there be light, and there was light' " (Gen. 1:3). "And God said, 'Let us make man' " (Gen. 1:26). By the effortless spoken word of God, he brought into being what had previously not existed. No other ancient creation story describes creation in such fashion.

We usually limit the creative activity of God to a remote primordial past. However, we can still observe the creative activity of God's word at work in the world today. Every time a person is confronted with the gospel, whether he reads it or hears it from a friend or a preacher, and accepts its claims that Jesus is the Son of God and his Savior, the creative activity of God's word is actualized in his experience. New Testament language describing the conversion experience also reflects this belief about the creative activity of God's word in terms such as "born again" (John 3:7), "regeneration" (Titus 3:5), "new creation" (2 Cor. 5:17, RSV). A person's salvation is the creation story through the word of God all over again.

When John said, "In the beginning was the Word [Greek, *logos*] and the Word was with God and the Word was God" (John 1:1), he was not describing Jesus in Greek philosophical concepts. John was a Jew and spoke out of a background of Jewish beliefs about words. What more apt term could he have used to sum up the qualities of Jesus Christ than "the Word"? His hearers would have understood that he was describing Jesus as living, powerful, and the Creator.

When the Old Testament prophets proclaimed, "Thus says the Lord," the note of authority was there because they believed that God's word was able to accomplish what he said. Is it any wonder that they were possessed by God's word and felt compelled to speak it, even at the risk of losing their lives?

He Was Possessed by God's Spirit

The Old Testament speaks frequently of the Spirit of God (approximately 232 times). The Hebrew word for "spirit" is *ruach,* the same word that in other contexts can be translated as "wind" (Gen. 8:1) or "breath" (Job 12:10). In an obvious play on words we are told that the prophets were possessed by the Spirit *(ruach),* but the words of false prophets were only wind *(ruach)* (Jer. 5:13; see also Mic. 2:11). The use of a word that can mean both "wind" and "Spirit" suggests the awesome power manifested by the presence of God.

The term "Holy Spirit" is found in only three verses in the Old Testament (Ps. 51:11; Isa. 63:10-11). It is, therefore, a distinctively New Testament emphasis,[2] though the holiness of God is frequently affirmed in the Old Testament.

The activity of the Spirit seems to be different in the Old Testament from that described in the New Testament. The New Testament speaks of the sealing of the Holy Spirit (Eph. 1:13; 4:30) and the indwelling of the Spirit (1 Cor. 3:16; Rom. 8:9). The Old Testament, however, suggests that the Spirit came upon a person to empower him for a certain task. The judges were endued with military prowess or unusual strength (Judg. 6:34; 11:29; 14:19). Bezalel was given craftsmanship for the work of the tabernacle (Ex. 31:3). Prophets, priests, and kings were possessed by the Spirit (Num. 11:25; 2 Chron. 15:1; 24:20; 36:22).

The Spirit could depart when the task was completed or if the person were disobedient (Samson, Judg. 16:20; Saul, 1 Sam. 16:14). The New Testament equivalent for the sense of loss of God's presence is "quenching" the Spirit (1 Thess. 5:19).

The prophets did not speak frequently of the activity of the Spirit, but it is obvious that they had experienced it (Isa. 48:16; 59:21; Ezek. 3:12; Mic. 3:8). In a significant statement Zechariah acknowledged that the word of the Lord came through the prophets by his Spirit (Zech. 7:12).

Though Saul was not among the prophets, the Spirit of the Lord came upon him mightily as a confirmation sign that he had been chosen by God as king. He began to prophesy, and people asked if he were among the prophets (1 Sam. 10:10-11; compare

19:24). His unusual behavior was reminiscent of the ecstatic behavior of prophets associated with Spirit possession. Later the Spirit departed from Saul and left him a tormented, half-crazed man (1 Sam. 16:14), consumed by a desire to kill his rival David.

Isaiah described the experience of Spirit possession in these words: "The Spirit of the Sovereign Lord is on me,/because the Lord has anointed me" (Isa. 61:1, NIV: compare Jahaziel, 2 Chron. 20:14). When Ezekiel was called, he acknowledged that the Spirit had entered him (Ezek. 2:2). On occasions he said that the Spirit transported him from one place to another (3:12-15; 8:3; 37:1). Zechariah equated accomplishment of the Lord's work with the Spirit: "Not by might, nor by power, but by my Spirit" (Zech. 4:6). On another occasion this same prophet affirmed that the Lord had sent his words to earlier prophets by the Spirit (Zech. 7:12). Concerning another Zechariah, son of Jehoiada the priest, it is said that the Spirit of God "came upon" (literally "clothed") him (2 Chron. 24:20, KJV).

The prophets were self-effacing, without ambition for personal honor or power. They only desired to be God's spokesmen. The quality of humility is characteristic of the work of the Spirit described in the New Testament: "He will not speak on His own initiative, . . . He shall glorify Me" (John 16:13-14, NASB).

Spirit possession was a positive evidence that a man was a true prophet. However, it also is a difficult test to apply objectively to another person. Ecstatic, weird behavior was characteristic of false prophets and actually bolstered the people's confidence in them. But bizarre conduct cannot be attributed to the Spirit of God, though it is sometimes confused with Spirit activity and possession.

The Moral Life of the Prophet
Was Consistent with God's Standards

At Mount Sinai the Lord admonished his people: "You shall be holy, for I the LORD your God am holy" (Lev. 19:2, NASB). There is probably no biblical word more misunderstood than "holy." Unfortunately, it has largely lost its real meaning. Popularly, it is frequently associated with a "holier-than-thou" attitude that is far removed from its biblical usage. In the ancient Near East "holy" did not have the moral and ethical content it came to have when associated with Israel's God. The word literally means to cut or to separate. Therefore, prostitutes who served in the pagan temples were called "holy ones." It simply meant that they were set apart or dedicated to serve their deities in the temple. We would call their conduct immoral, even though it was done in the name of religion.

The people of Israel rarely exhibited the quality of holiness that God expected of them, but the prophets did. In order for them to call the people back to the law of God, their own lives had to be above reproach. Though the people accused the prophets of many things, they did not accuse them of immorality or hypocritical double standards.

The requirement of personal purity is best exemplified in Isaiah's call experience. In the presence of a holy and righteous God, Isaiah was overwhelmed with his own unworthiness and sinfulness. He cried out, "Woe is me, for I am undone" (KJV). God responded by having one of the seraphim touch Isaiah's lips with a burning coal from the altar. The act served as a symbol that the prophet had been purged and purified and was now fit to be God's spokesman (Isa. 6:5-7).

Unfortunately, our age has been subjected all too often to self-appointed spokesmen for God who go about the country making a show of piety. They bilk trusting people of their money and then depart to spend the money on "wine, women, and song." At least this is the popular caricature of the minister that is nurtured in today's literature. The book *Elmer Gantry* has probably destroyed the trust of more people in the minister than any other single piece of literature in modern times.

The media usually portray the minister as stupid, weak, insensitive, dishonest, and frequently immoral. Unfortunately, there are enough ministers like this to justify the accusation, though they represent only a small minority. The Old Testament prophets would have called these people "false prophets," for they understood that God required the highest standards of personal morality of anyone who would be his spokesman (Jer. 29:21-23).

As with the other tests of the true prophet which have already been examined, this one is valid. It is not, however, always easy to apply because a self-proclaimed "prophet" may hide behind a mask of piety and deceive many people.

The Moral Content of the Message
Was Consistent with God's Nature

If the moral life of the prophet was consistent with God's standards of morality, it follows that his messages would be consistent with God's nature. God would never instruct a prophet to do anything that was inconsistent with God's own nature. Nor would a prophet encourage his listeners to do anything contrary to God's nature.

If a legitimate test of the true prophet is that he reflects the nature of God, how can we know what the nature of God is? The answer is that his nature has been revealed in the pages of the Scriptures. If we want to know what God is like, we find his characteristics there—holy, righteous, loving, compassionate, patient, and longsuffering, to name a few.

Rarely a month goes by that the newspapers do not contain the account of a person who has killed someone or committed some other gross act of immorality. He then justifies his act by saying, "God told me to do it." God never tells anyone to do something that is contrary to his Word. His Word says, "Thou shalt not kill . . . Thou shalt not commit adultery," and so on. He will never make an exception for any individual. Whatever influences a person to commit an immoral act, it is not God.

God is concerned for the poor, the oppressed, and the exploited. He is concerned about racial injustice, misuse of the gift of sex, and greed that expresses itself through war and other forms of violence. He is concerned about anything that degrades the human creature made in God's image, such as drugs that destroy the body or pornography that destroys moral sensitivity. These same concerns will be reflected in the messages of the true prophet of God today.

The test of moral content of the message is more objective than some of the other tests we have examined and easier to apply. However, it is possible to speak favorably on moral issues but not actually be a spokesman for God. There are people who are deeply concerned about poverty, racial injustice, war, and other ethical issues who speak more effectively on these matters than Christians. Yet these same people may at the same time deny the existence of God. Their morality is selective—that is, for them a deed may be moral in one situation and immoral in another. They become their own judges of what is right and wrong.

As examples of this myopic concept of morality, some people condemned the involvement of the United States in the war in Vietnam but did not speak against Vietnamese aggression in Cambodia. Nor did they speak out against Russian aggression in Czechoslovakia, Cuban aggression in Angola, or Chinese aggression in Vietnam. They were vocal about atrocities committed by one side but mute about atrocities committed by the other. They deplore racial prejudice of whites toward other races but refuse to condemn similar prejudice when it comes from the other direction. They speak out about the violation of any human rights in this country but prefer to say nothing about worse violations in Communist-dominated countries. They condemn dishonest acts by another political party but prefer to cover up similar transgressions in their own party. They want total freedom of expression for themselves but would restrict the freedom of those with opposing views, given the opportunity.

The list of these moral flipflops is endless. The Old Testament prophets could never have been accused of such moral duplicity because they believed in the absolutes of God's moral laws. If an act or a thought is wrong for one person, they would have said it is wrong for everyone. The ills of this or any other country will never be solved until a single standard of morality—God's standard—is applied to all situations.

He Did Not Preach from Personal Ambition

In the study of the calls of the prophets (chap. 1) it was pointed out that none of them sat down and deliberately decided that he would be a prophet because of good pay, short hours, and excellent opportunities for personal advancement. In fact, it was only the divine compulsion that enabled them to accept the prophetic mantle.

Amos denied the charge that he preached for pay (Amos 7:14), after Amaziah told him to return to Judah where the people would pay for the kind of messages Amos was preaching (7:12).[3] Jeremiah summed up the attitude of the false prophets with the accusation: "For from the least of them even to the greatest of them,/Every one is greedy for gain,/And from the prophet even to the priest/Every one deals falsely./And they have healed the wound of My people slightly,/Saying, 'Peace, peace,'/But there is no peace./Were they ashamed because of the abomination they have done?/They were not even ashamed at all;/They did not even know how to blush" (Jer. 6:13-15a, NASB). For such truthfulness prophets were often rewarded with persecution (1 Kings 22:27; 2 Chron. 36:16; Jer. 37:15) or even death (Matt. 23:30-31).

Perhaps all the blame should not be directed against the false prophets for their lying words. The people demanded pleasing, reassuring messages. It was a kind of community-pressured blackmail that caused the prophet to prostitute his integrity to remain in favor with his people. A twentieth-century application is the church that will not pay the salary of a preacher who exposes the sins of his congregation. He is told to conform or risk losing his job.

God's word should not be for sale to the highest bidder. When it is, the integrity of the spokesman is forfeited. He who pays the piper will call the tune. The prophets understood the danger of speaking only what the people wanted to hear. When pressure was brought to bear on Micaiah to speak pleasing words to the king, the prophet replied, "What the LORD says to me, that will I speak" (1 Kings 22:14, NASB). Ezekiel spoke about prophets who delivered pleasing messages to those who paid them but had only curses for those who would not (Ezek. 13:17-19; see also Jer. 4:10; 6:13-14).

The faith healer who demands to be paid for his services, the evangelist in "mod" clothing who travels with his entourage in a private airplane, or the pastor who accepts the call of the church that pays the largest salary may be the kinsman of those false prophets who were condemned in the Old Testament because they preached from personal ambition. How few pastors feel "called" to go to a smaller church than where they are presently serving! The New Testament declares that the person who devotes his life to the proclamation of the Word of God is worthy to be supported (Luke 10:7). However, an ambitious person who seeks fame and fortune through the ministry often brings dishonor to it.

His Message Was Frequently Unpopular

The prophets saw that Israel's faithlessness was leading to national ruin. Therefore, they did not hesitate to name the sins that were bringing the wrath of God upon the nation. They were critics of their times and wanted to bring reform to Israel. They warned and pleaded; their words were not designed to bring false comfort or to entertain the people. Their messages could be redemptive if heeded, for they always had Israel's welfare at heart.

Such messages were rarely well received because of the human disposition not to want to be reminded of our sins. It has been facetiously said (but with an element of truth) that if the prophet's messages pleased the privileged classes—the exploiters and oppressors of the poor—he could not be a true prophet.

This does not mean that a true spokesman of God can only speak condemning words. There is a place for encouragement and comfort. Every one of the prophets not only preached messages of doom but also messages of hope and encouragement. Some Old Testament scholars have insisted that the same prophet could not deliver messages both of doom and of hope. Therefore, where both messages occur, these scholars conclude they must have been spoken by different men. However, the supportive message was just as much the word of God for Israel as the condemning message.

Both Jeremiah and Ezekiel constantly preached messages that warned of the coming destruction of Jerusalem. But when the city finally fell in 587 BC they did not spend the rest of their days saying to the people, "I told you so!" (Admittedly, one who had been sorely abused might be tempted to do so.) They immediately changed their emphasis from judgment and spoke about the glorious future that God had in store for his people.

After the destruction of Jerusalem, those who survived seemed to be convinced that Jeremiah was truly a prophet of God. Therefore, they came to him and promised to do whatever "The LORD your God may tell us the way in which we should walk and the thing that we should do. . . . May the LORD be a true and faithful witness against us, if we do not act in accordance with the whole message with which the LORD your God will send you to us" (Jer. 42:3,5, NASB).

It might appear they had learned their lesson, but such a conclusion would be erroneous. For when Jeremiah did tell them what to do, his advice was not what they wanted to hear. Therefore, their leaders responded, "You are telling a lie! The LORD our God has not sent you to say . . ." (Jer. 43:2, NASB).

The prophet was usually greeted with a negative response to his unpopular messages. At times he wished that he could speak words that would ingratiate him with the people. Jeremiah was concerned that every time he opened his mouth only words of doom came out (Jer. 20:8). King Ahab complained to King Jehoshaphat concerning the prophet Micaiah: "I hate him, because he does not prophesy good concerning me, but evil" (1 Kings 22:8, NASB).

No true prophet of God delighted to tell his people the awful fate that lay in store for them if they continued to disobey God. The preacher who discovers that he enjoys denouncing his congregation for its failures should examine his ministry. A true prophet delivers a word of judgment with a broken heart. He is a shepherd who loves the sheep (Jer. 10:1-15; see also Ezek. 34:1-22; John 10:14-15).

False prophets were like quack physicians covering over a cancer with an adhesive bandage (Jer. 6:14). They were compared to plasterers covering over a flimsily constructed wall that would topple with the first heavy rain (Ezek. 13:11-14). They announced peace when there was no peace because that was what the people wanted to hear (Jer. 6:14; Ezek. 13:10). The prophet of God could never prostitute his messages just to be popular.

The Inner Witness of the Holy Spirit

Each of the tests discussed thus far is a valid test of a true prophet. However, in each case it is difficult to apply these tests objectively in order to know whether a person is a true or false prophet.

Some Old Testament scholars have concluded that there is no infallible test to distinguish a true from a false prophet. However, there is a way to know whether the message is from God. The power and presence of the Spirit in the message can be identified by the inner witness of the Holy Spirit. "The Spirit himself testifies with our spirit that we are God's children" (Rom. 8:16, NIV). That same Spirit can be called upon to distinguish between the true and the false prophet.

Some will respond to this line of reasoning by saying that it is mystical, nonscholarly, and quite subjective. Even Jesus admitted that it is difficult to pin down the activity of the Spirit. He said to Nicodemus: "The wind blows wherever it pleases. You may hear its sound, but you cannot tell where it comes from or where it is going. So it is with everyone born of the Spirit" (John 3:8, NIV). The Spirit is as elusive as the wind but also just as self-revealing.

The Christian can be guided by the Spirit (Matt. 4:1; Rom. 8:14). He must preserve a sensitivity to the "still small voice" (1 Kings 19:12) by not quenching the work of the Spirit (1 Thess. 5:19). A life of obedience, faithfulness, and constant confession of sin will maintain the unbroken flow of the power and guidance of the Holy Spirit for the believer.

We are exhorted to "test the spirits to see whether they are from God" (1 John 4:1, NIV). This appeal implies that it is possible to know whether a person is speaking God's word through the Spirit of God (Zech. 7:12) or through the deceit of his own heart (Jer. 14:14; 23:21; 27:15; Ezek. 13:17). First Corinthians 2:11 adds further encouragement that we may know if the words are from the Lord: "No one knows the thoughts of God except the Spirit of God" (NIV).

Conclusion

If a person appears among us today and claims to have a message from God, we ought to listen to him if he truly is a spokesman from God. Just as emphatically, we should not listen to him if his words are not from the Lord. Ancient Israel and Judah were unable to recognize the true prophetic voices that warned them to turn back to God to avert destruction. Since they refused to turn back, the result was national ruin.

From time to time the word of the Lord may come to us as a nation or to an individual through a modern-day prophet. We ought to be able to learn some lessons from the history of Israel. If the message is from God, we should recognize the authority behind the message and then obey it.

Notes

1. Compare the Septuagint translation of the Old Testament, where "prophet" is sometimes translated "false prophet"—for example, Jeremiah 27:9; 29:1.

2. It is found approximately ninety times in the New Testament.

3. The word used by Amos to suggest pay is "bread." The word has come full circle to mean money in today's slang! In Amos' day "bread" was synonymous for food in general.

"Whether They Hear or Not"
(The Message of the Prophet)

The most important element of Old Testament prophecy was the message of the prophet. Men and women from differing backgrounds appeared from time to time before the people of Israel with the claim that God had spoken to them. They felt obligated to communicate these messages to their countrymen, whether their hearers responded favorably or not. There is a timeless quality in their messages that is never exhausted, even by the most intensive study.

How the Message Was Received

Because God is sovereign, he is not limited to one mode of revelation. "In the past God spoke . . . through the prophets at many times and in various ways" (Heb. 1:1, NIV). Some of the "various ways" by which God gave his messages to the prophets will be examined in this chapter.

The Audible Voice

The prophets frequently introduced their oracles with words such as "The word of the Lord came to . . . saying," "This is what the Lord says," or "Says the Lord." How are we to understand statements that suggest God speaking to particular men? We need not insist that God spoke in an audible voice or in the Hebrew language. Communication between God and prophet could have occurred in some other way. However, we should immediately add that it would be unwise to place any restrictions on the manner in which God might choose to speak. The fact that Paul's traveling companions heard a voice on the Damascus road, though they saw no one, suggests that revelation was sometimes audible (Acts 9:7).

However, it is more likely that "hearing" a divine oracle should be compared to the experience of a person today who says, "God spoke to me." He usually does not mean that he has heard an audible voice; but the experience of hearing is, nevertheless, quite real. God usually speaks through the "still, small voice" (1 Kings 19:12).

Dreams

Though the Old Testament emphasizes spoken revelation, it also includes a number of other ways the prophets received their messages.

Dreams were a common mode of revelation, both in Israel and in the ancient Near East (for example, Job 33:14-15; 1 Sam. 28:6). Dreams are especially prominent in the books of Genesis (Gen. 28:12; 37:5,9; 40:5) and Daniel (Dan. 2,4,7). The prophets were linked with dreams in Deuteronomy 13:1. This passage does not deny that dreams were a valid means of receiving oracles. Its purpose was to warn that any revelation, however received, was invalid if the prophet also said, "Let us go after other gods" (Deut. 13:2). In Numbers 12:6-8 the Lord ranked dreams as a less important mode of revelation than "mouth to mouth" (Num. 12:8). Saul tried desperately to obtain a word from the Lord before engaging in battle with the Philistines, but every method failed, including dreams. God refused to speak to him (1 Sam. 28:6). Joel predicted that "your sons and your daughters shall prophesy,/your old men shall dream dreams" (Joel 2:28).

Dreams as revelations were not limited to the prophets. Nebuchadnezzar, king of Babylon, had dreams that troubled him, but he could not interpret them. Daniel was called in; and because he was able to interpret the king's dreams, he was promoted to a high position in the Babylonian court (Dan. 2; see also chap. 4). Daniel himself also experienced revelatory dreams (Dan. 7:1).

Jeremiah minimized dreams as a means of revelation: "Let the prophet who has a dream tell the dream, but let him who has my word speak my word faithfully. What has straw in common with wheat?" (Jer. 23:28). He equated dreams with lying prophets (Jer. 23:25,27,32; see also Zech. 10:2). On another occasion he warned the people not to listen to "your prophets, your diviners, your dreamers" (Jer. 27:9; see also 29:8-9) because what they were saying was a lie (27:10).

One must never place restrictions on God, but dependence on dreams for revelation can be dangerous. One's bizarre dreams could be attributed to a cheese sandwich eaten just before retiring rather than to divine revelation!

Visions

The vision was another common means of communicating the divine oracle to the prophet. Some Old Testament scholars interpret the vision as an ecstatic experience. They suggest that visions were self-induced by concentration, vigorous gyrations (like a whirling dervish), or even hallucinogenic drugs! It is true that many of the prophets had visions, but it does not follow that they were in some kind of abnormal, uncontrollable state at the time.

The opening words of the book of Amos may give the best clue to the true nature of prophetic visions: "The words of Amos . . . which he saw concerning Israel" (Amos 1:1). Habakkuk begins with similar words: "The oracle which Habakkuk the prophet saw" (Hab. 1:1, NASB). Whatever the unusual phrase means, it does link the vision with hearing a word from God.

The visions of the prophets were not hallucinatory even in the strictest sense of the word, for they were always accompanied by the spoken word.

More than any other prophet Ezekiel is associated with visions. His call began with a vision of God in a storm cloud

(Ezek. 1:1 to 3:15). He was carried to Jerusalem in a vision where he saw abominable religious practices taking place within the Temple itself (8:1-18). In a vision he saw a valley filled with dry bones (37:1-14). The book closes with an extensive vision describing a restored Temple and Temple community (40:1 to 48:35).

Running a close second to Ezekiel in the number of visions experienced was Daniel. His visions were the most bizarre of all, replete with horned animals and supernatural beings (Dan. 7—12). His visions are interpreted by some Old Testament scholars as examples of an apocalyptic literary form rather than literal experiences and by others as a blueprint for the ages.

Other prophets especially associated with visionary experiences include Amos (a series of five visions, Amos 7:1-9; 8:1-3; 9:1), Jeremiah (a rod of almond, Jer. 1:11-12; a boiling pot, 1:13-16; two baskets of figs, 24:1-10), and Zechariah. This prophet experienced a series of eight visions, some in color (Zech. 1:7 to 6:8).

Teraphim

Less frequently encountered modes of revelation include the teraphim, or household gods (Gen. 31:30). The size and shape of these figurines is not known. They may have been small carved representations of the deity (Gen. 31:19,34-35) or life-size models (1 Sam. 19:13,16). Nor can it be determined how the teraphim were consulted to receive the divine revelation.

Zechariah 10:2 warned that the teraphim spoke "nonsense" (the Hebrew word literally means "trouble" or "sorrow"). The teraphim were probably never recognized in Israel as a legitimate mode of revelation (1 Sam. 15:23; 2 Kings 23:24), though frequently consulted elsewhere (Ezek. 21:21).

The Ephod

The teraphim and ephod are sometimes linked together (Judg. 17:5; 18:14-20). The latter was a priestly garment of some kind

(Ex. 25:7; 28:4; 1 Sam. 22:18). It was used by the priests to receive divine direction (1 Sam. 14:3,18;¹ 23:9; 30:7-8). There is no evidence to indicate that the prophets also used the ephod to obtain messages from God.

The Urim and Thummim

Sometimes the will of God was determined by consulting the Urim and Thummim (Num. 27:21; Deut. 33:8; 1 Sam. 14:41; 28:6; Ezra 2:63). Though there is much uncertainty about the appearance and function of the urim and thummim, they were likely two stones that decorated the priest's garment (Ex. 28:30; Lev. 8:8). By some mechanical means they could be used to obtain an answer from the deity. It has been suggested that the urim produced a negative answer since it comes from a Hebrew word meaning "curse." The thummim probably gave a positive answer since it comes from a word meaning "perfection."

If the stones did represent negative and positive answers, questions had to be worded in such a way that they could be answered with yes or no. Perhaps the priest would place the two stones in a pouch, ask the question, then reach his hand into the pouch and draw out a stone. The stone drawn indicated a positive or negative answer to the question.

Casting Lots

The will of God was frequently determined by casting lots. The lot was used to make some very important decisions in Israel. Lots were cast to determine the division of land among the Israelite tribes (Josh. 14:1-2). Saul was chosen as Israel's first king by casting lots (1 Sam. 10:20-21). Sailors cast lots that pointed to Jonah as the culprit responsible for a storm that was about to engulf their boat (Jonah 1:7). The practice continued into New Testament times when the apostle to replace Judas was chosen by lots (Acts 1:23-26).

The casting of lots to determine God's will was honored on

occasions, but it is a practice that should not be encouraged. The modern parallel to this mechanical means of determining God's will is the use of the Bible to give answers. A person takes Bible in hand, closes his eyes, and offers a brief prayer. He then flips the Bible open and accepts as guidance from the Lord the first verse on which his finger falls. Of course, if he is not satisfied with the verse (particularly if it happens to be a genealogical listing such as Gen. 36:42), he may try for two out of three! Seriously, though, it should be acknowledged that God has on occasion honored this method of seeking his will, as many sincere Christians would testify.

Theophany

Revelation sometimes came as a theophany.[2] God appeared to Abraham as a man and told him about the impending judgment on Sodom (Gen. 18:1-3,20). He appeared to Moses in a burning bush and there spoke to him (Ex. 3:2-6). He appeared to Solomon in a dream by night (1 Kings 3:5). He appeared to Isaiah in the Temple (Isa. 6) and to Ezekiel seated upon a throne in the midst of a storm cloud (Ezek. 1:26-28). God never appears in the Bible in the form of an animal, though deities were frequently depicted in animal form in other ancient Near Eastern religions.

Rational Explanations

Some have overrationalized the phenomenon of prophecy, thereby eliminating its uniqueness. They describe the prophets only as men who had unusual ability to discern the contemporary historical scene, who could see "the handwriting on the wall," so to speak. The rationalists argue that the prophets drew their conclusions about what was going to happen from their observation of current events and their understanding of God's nature. For the rationalist there is nothing unique about prophecy, but we agree with those who insist that the prophetic consciousness "is one of hearing what God says to the prophet, not one of diagnosing the forces and probabilities inherent in the historical situation."[3]

The prophet heard God speak; then he repeated that message to the people. Habakkuk was distinctive among the prophets because he took questions to God instead of only taking messages from God to the people (Hab. 1:2-4,12-17).

How the Message Was Transmitted to Others

By the Spirit

Biblical writers constantly remind us that the prophetic message was transmitted by the Spirit of God. The Spirit came upon the seventy elders chosen by Moses, and they prophesied (Num. 11:16-17,24-25). Eldad and Medad were not present when the seventy received the prophetic Spirit; but when the Spirit came to rest on them, they also prophesied (Num. 11:26-29). Samuel told Saul that he would meet a band of prophets. At that time the Spirit of the Lord would come mightily upon him and he would begin to prophesy with them (1 Sam. 10:6,10-11). Hosea described the popular reaction to the Spirit-filled prophets: "The prophet is a fool, the man of the spirit is mad" (Hos. 9:7). Joel said that sons and daughters would prophesy when the Spirit was poured out on them (Joel 2:28). Micah declared that he was filled "with power—with the Spirit of the LORD" (Mic. 3:8, NASB). It was the Spirit that lifted up Ezekiel and carried him to Jerusalem (Ezek. 8:3) and later brought him to the valley of dry bones (Ezek. 37:1). Much later the Levites, while confessing the sins of the people in prayer, acknowledged that for many years God had warned his people by his Spirit through the prophets (Neh. 9:30).

In one of the older studies of the prophets the statement was made that the greatest quality of the prophets was that they were "masters of the art of persuasive speech."[4] However, if the prophet had been asked, he would have insisted that it was the power of the Spirit that swayed the people (see Jer. 1:9-10; Zech. 4:6). Both Moses (Ex. 4:10) and Jeremiah (Jer. 1:6) denied being public speakers.

Oral Proclamation

The prophets usually transmitted the messages they had received by calling the people together and proclaiming the message aloud. Moses was to have been the mouthpiece of the Lord, relaying the divine oracles to the people. However, because of his refusal to serve as the spokesman, God used Aaron his brother as a substitute. He would continue speaking to Moses, who would repeat the message to Aaron. Aaron, in turn, would carry the word to all the people (Ex. 4:15-16). Sometimes a prophet spoke to large groups (Jer. 7:2; 11:1-2), but frequently he took his message to one individual (Jer. 38:14-26).

The Written Message

It is impossible from our distance to know how many of the prophets wrote down their own messages either before or after delivering them. Without doubt some of them recorded their oracles. A number of the prophets were historians and were accustomed by training and disposition to record carefully the events to which they were witnesses. Nathan recorded the history of the reigns of David and Solomon, though there is no evidence that he recorded his own oracles (1 Chron. 29:29; 2 Chron. 9:29). Other prophets who kept historical records were Ahijah the Shilonite (2 Chron. 9:29); Iddo the seer (2 Chron. 9:29); Shemaiah (2 Chron. 12:15); Iddo (2 Chron. 13:22); and Isaiah (2 Chron. 26:22).

Jeremiah 36 gives the most detailed description of how a prophet preserved his messages. Jeremiah dictated to his scribe Baruch all the prophecies he could remember from the previous twenty-two years. The written messages were taken to King Jehoiakim, who scornfully burned them in the fire. When Jeremiah heard that the king had destroyed the oracles, he called

Baruch and dictated them again. The second time he remembered some others he had not dictated the first time to his scribe.
Therefore, we must be grateful to a king's anger for some of Jeremiah's messages that otherwise might not have been recorded!

Other prophets did not write down their messages; their only
concern was to proclaim them. However, among the people
were those who heard the messages and carefully wrote them
down. It is probably inaccurate to call these recorders "disciples"
of the prophet, as many Old Testament scholars have done, for
in most cases the prophets seem not to have had any following
and to have had very few friends.[5] It is impossible to trace with
certainty the complex process or to understand the means of
transmission and preservation of the prophetic oracles.[6] We can
only affirm that they were preserved by divine providence.
Unless we can make this affirmation, we would be obliged to
forfeit the divine inspiration and reliability of the messages in the
form we have them today.

Scholars once believed that all the messages were transmitted
orally until postexilic times. Today, however, there is a prevail-
ing attitude that from the earliest period, many of the prophets
wrote down their own sayings.[7]

Symbolic Acts

The spoken message of a prophet was sometimes accompanied
by a symbolic act (also called an "enacted parable"). The
prophet would reenact the message in "miniature" and then
explain his act to the people. Saul tore the garment of Samuel as
the prophet turned away from the king. Samuel used the acci-
dent as a symbolic act to announce that the kingdom was being
torn away from Saul (1 Sam. 15:27-28).

However, symbolic acts were usually deliberately staged by
the prophet. Ahijah tore a new garment he was wearing to
announce to Jeroboam the division of the kingdom at Solomon's
death (1 Kings 11:29-32). The prophets who most frequently

used symbolic acts as a mode of transmitting their messages were Jeremiah* and Ezekiel.* The false prophets also used symbolic acts (2 Chron. 18:10; Jer. 28:10-11).

Spoken Parables

Prophets also frequently communicated their oracles in the form of spoken parables (Hos. 12:10). The parable was a popular form of the storyteller's art that appealed to the people. It was a brief narrative that taught a single idea. Examples of the prophetic parable are found in 2 Samuel 12:1-4 and Isaiah 5:1-7. Parables are especially prominent in Ezekiel (15:1-8; 16:1-63; 17:1-24; 23:1-49; 24:1-14). They epitomized a favorite teaching method used by Jesus.

The entire book of Jonah has been interpreted by some as being a parable rather than a literal, historical experience. If it is a parable, it violates three common characteristics of parables found elsewhere: (1) the parable was usually brief; (2) it did not ordinarily use well-known historical figures; (3) its interpretation was always given. Jonah does not fit any of these criteria. As prophecy Jonah is unique because it does not contain oracles proclaimed by the prophet, except for the brief "forty days, and Nineveh shall be overthrown" (3:4). It is, rather, an account of the experiences of Jonah.

It is not our purpose here to enter into the discussion of the problems associated with the interpretation of the book of Jonah. Some scholars have been unwilling to accept the story as historical. However, whether understood as a historical event or as a parable, the Bible student extracts the message of the story parabolically. That is, he asks what the story teaches. It teaches that Jonah represented an Israel that was unwilling to share its God with other peoples. The Bible student who insists on the historicity of Jonah is not required to abandon that position in order to interpret the book parabolically. If he does, it is on other grounds.

The Names of Children

One other way by which the prophetic message was transmitted should be mentioned, if only because it seems so strange
to us. Occasionally the prophetic message was proclaimed
through the names the prophet gave his children. The names of
Hosea's children describe the progression of the breakdown in
the covenant relationship between God and his people. The first
child was called Jezreel, which means "God scatters." The second born was Lo-ruhamah, which means "No pity," and the
third was Lo-ammi, "Not my people" (Hos. 1:4,6,9, KJV). The
names tell us that God would punish his people and finally deny
them as his own covenant people.

Isaiah gave names to his two sons that have been interpreted
as messages of judgment. Others understand that one name contained a message of judgment and the other a message of hope
for the future. The first son was Shear-jashub (Isa. 7:3), which
means "a remnant shall return." Interpreted as judgment, it was
a warning of almost total destruction of Israel. Interpreted as
hope, it said a remnant of the nation would survive. The other
son was called Maher-shalal-hashbaz (Isa. 8:3-4), which means
"speed the spoil, hasten the prey." Clearly his name contained a
warning of imminent judgment for Israel.

Kinds of Prophetic Messages

The prophets spoke to every kind of situation. Sometimes
their messages announced inescapable doom (Jer. 15:1; Ezek.
14:14; Hos. 13:8; Amos 5:18-20; 6:7-8). Sometimes they gave
warnings accompanied by appeals to repent and to return to the
Lord before it was too late (Amos 5:6; Jer. 3:12-14; 38:17-18).

Intercession

Prophets did not enjoy announcing the doom of their people
(Jer. 13:17; 23:9). Consequently, they were frequently found
interceding with God not to inflict the judgment he had asked
them to announce. Among the prophets noted as intercessors

were Moses (Ex. 32:11,30-32; Num. 14:13-19), Samuel (1 Sam. 12:19-23), and Jeremiah (Jer. 15:11; 18:20). Sometimes God was swayed by their appeals (Ex. 32:11-14; Amos 7:1-6). At other times he told them it would do no good to intercede (Jer. 7:16; 11:14; 14:11).

Messages Against Foreign Nations

All of the major and minor prophets with the exception of Hosea preached messages against foreign nations. Some of these messages were quite lengthy and included a number of nations (Amos 1—2; Isa. 13—23; Jer. 46—51; Ezek. 25—32). Others were very brief and were directed against only one or two nations (Joel 3:4-8; Obad.; Mic. 5:5-9; Zeph. 2:4-15).

There is never a hint that the prophets took the messages directly to the foreign nations for whom they were intended or that they instructed anyone else to do so (except Jer. 51:59-64). It was considered enough to announce the message, for it was believed that the word, once spoken, was potent. The word itself would bring about the fulfillment of the curses or blessings that had been pronounced. Also, the message could have reached the nations through representatives of other countries who were in Jerusalem (Jer. 25:17-26; 27:3). They would hear the messages spoken against their land and, in turn, carry them back to their own people.

If the primary purpose of the messages against foreign nations was not to announce judgment in a face-to-face encounter, what was their purpose? One answer is that the message would serve to get the attention of Israelite audiences. When Amos journeyed to Israel and began announcing judgment upon Damascus, Philistia, Tyre, Edom, Ammon, Moab, and even upon Judah, he attracted a large, enthusiastic audience. When he turned on Israel with a stern message of judgment, only then did his Israelite audience understand that everything said to that point was leading up to judgment upon them (Amos 2:6-8). But at least he had gotten their attention!

Messages against foreign nations also served as warnings to Israel and Judah. These messages made it clear that God was going to bring judgment on peoples who did not pretend to believe in him and did not enjoy a covenant relationship with him. If so, how much more Israel and Judah, the recipients of God's covenant blessings, could expect judgment to fall on them.

A final purpose of the messages against foreign nations, strangely enough, was to bring comfort and assurance to Israel and Judah. How? By reminding them that God had not forgotten them and that he was going to punish those nations that had mistreated and abused his people. Christians through the centuries have found comfort in knowing that one day God will bring judgment on the wicked of the world (Rev. 21).

Very few people bother to read the prophets' messages against other nations because somehow they do not seem as theologically significant as those spoken to Israel or to Judah. Even the person committed to reading "straight through the Bible" tends to pass over these passages. However, their theological content is rich and varied and should not be ignored. They teach the sovereignty of God—he is the Creator of all peoples and has the right to judge them. They teach the universality of God—he is the God of all nations and ultimately must be recognized by them. They also show that the moral laws of God have universal validity—God will judge all nations for violating his moral laws just as he will judge Israel and Judah.

These passages are given little attention also because they seem extremely nationalistic and vengeful. They seem to rejoice over the anticipated punishment of Israel's enemies. Some people are perturbed by the fact that God used the Israelites to destroy the Canaanites. But they are not troubled when he used the Babylonians to punish the Israelites. The principle is the same. God will punish wickedness wherever he finds it, and he frequently uses human instruments to do it. No nation can escape the judgment of God.

One final reason for the neglect of the messages against foreign nations is that they are about little-known places and events. Consequently, they seem to be of peripheral interest to a study of biblical history. However, since the foreign nations are given so much attention by so many of the prophets, these messages must be more important than generally acknowledged.

The Form of the Message

Preachers today vary the form of their sermons—at least they should! A steady diet of the introduction, three points, and conclusion format can become monotonous to a congregation. In contrast, the Old Testament prophets are characterized by the richness and variety of forms they used in communicating their messages. No questions need be raised about the inspiration of the Scriptures upon discovering that the prophets encased their messages in identifiable literary forms common to the ancient Near East. How else could they communicate in understandable fashion to their people, except against the background of their own culture?

They used poetry as well as prose to proclaim the divine revelation. In fact, all the prophetic books of the Old Testament contain poetry except Haggai and Malachi.

They spoke in parables (Isa. 5:1-7), riddles (Ezek. 17:2), and proverbs (Jer. 31:29). They used threats (Jer. 28:8), promises (Isa. 7:1-9), invectives (Amos 5:12), exhortations (Mal. 4:4), and warnings (Jer. 25:3-7). They used taunt songs (Isa. 37:22-29), dirges and laments (Hos. 6:1-3; the entire book of Lamentations). They also used love songs (Hos. 14:4-7), summons to battle (Joel 3:9-10), hymns (Isa. 25:1-5), and wisdom instruction (Jer. 17:7-8).

They borrowed the language of the courtroom to speak messages of judgment (Isa. 3:13-15; Amos 3:9; Hos. 4:1; Mic. 6:2; Jer. 25:31). They used the language of presentation at the royal court ("I am the Lord," Ezek. 6:10,13). They borrowed the words of the messenger who announced the king's decrees ("Thus says the Lord," Amos 2:4; Zech. 8:2; see also 2 Kings 18:19; 2 Chron. 32:10). The cry of woe, which had its origin in wailing for the dead, was frequently employed by the prophets (Isa. 5:8; Amos 5:18; Ezek. 13:3).

Form criticism is the discipline that first made a systematic study of the many forms of speech found in the Old Testament. It has been severely condemned by some Bible students as an attempt to discredit the Scriptures. Such a judgment shows misunderstanding of the positive values of form-critical studies. There have been excesses and errors, as is true with any study. Even some devotional studies have been guilty of seriously distorting the Scriptures. But the discovery that prophets and other Old Testament writers composed their messages in the literary forms common to the culture of their day should not surprise us. And that, essentially, is what form criticism has demonstrated.

It can easily be shown that we express ourselves in forms common to our cultural background. A business letter follows one form; a love letter, another. The two are easily distinguished! Rock music of the seventies is easily distinguished from the popular music of the thirties and forties.

The most common "form" of a sermon learned by first-year seminary students is an introduction, three points, and a conclusion. Sometimes a poem is added for a finishing touch! The fact that a preacher uses an established form for his sermon does not automatically make the sermon uninspired. The Holy Spirit can and does work through sermons that follow established forms. The discovery by form critics that the Old Testament prophets delivered their messages in the established forms of their times has helped place the prophets in the cultural context of their world.

Awareness of prophetic forms of speech in the Old Testament has been of positive benefit. It serves as a reminder that revelation is communicated through human instruments in understandable forms. Otherwise, the oracles of God would not be revelatory, but rather just the reverse.

Evaluation of the Success of the Prophet

If contemporary standards of success for the ministry were applied to the Old Testament prophets, they would have to be branded, almost without exception, as abysmal failures! Before rejecting this evaluation, one should ask: "What are our standards of success for ministers?" Candid answers to this question would include the following. The successful minister draws large crowds to hear him; the membership of his church increases year by year; the church is financially sound; he leads the people in impressive building programs. In short, he gets results. Further, he is a sought-after speaker at denominational meetings and at local clubs. He walks comfortably among the elite of the community. He is a dynamic orator; his sermons are entertaining and inspiring. He gets along well with the people in his church and community. His manners are polished. He dresses in the latest fashions; and, if quite daring, he may occasionally take part in a protest movement.

If these are the popular standards by which the success of today's minister is determined (and unfortunately they are), then we will have to write "Failure" across the names of the Old Testament prophets. The prophets did not get "results," if by "results" we mean that people listened to them and did what they demanded. No one listened to Amos, Hosea, Isaiah, Jeremiah, or Ezekiel. How do we know? If the people had listened, neither Israel nor Judah would have come under the judgment of God.

Only three prophets could be considered successful, if getting results is a measurement of success. Two of them were Haggai and Zechariah, who encouraged the people to start rebuilding the temple in 520 BC. Three weeks after Haggai made his first appeal, the people started laying the foundation (Hag. 1:12-15).

Any preacher who could stimulate his congregation to embark on a building program three weeks after his original appeal from the pulpit would have to be considered a success! The only other prophet who was "successful" was Jonah, and he was not even preaching to his own people but to the Ninevites. They repented at his preaching, and the city was not destroyed (Jonah 3:4-10).

By the standard of community acceptability and popularity, the Old Testament prophets would also have to be written off as failures. The prophet could not be separated from his message; and since the message was rejected, the prophet also was rejected. He knew loneliness, ridicule, physical abuse, imprisonment, and even death. He was not interested in making a name for himself. In fact, he frequently remained unnamed in the Scriptures (1 Kings 13:1-32; 20:13,28,35-43; 2 Kings 9:1-4; 21:10-15).[10]

However, we rebel at the suggestion that the prophets were failures. Instead, we insist that they were magnificent successes. They must not be judged as failures because the standards applied by God are not necessarily the standards we apply to determine success and failure. The Lord had only one criterion by which he measured a prophet: Was he obedient to God? Or, expressed another way: Did the prophet deliver the message that God gave him? If he did, then in God's records he was successful. The task of the prophet was not to get results or to achieve personal acceptance. His one task was to deliver the messages God gave him. He was not responsible or accountable for responses. Whether they heard or not, they would know that a prophet had been in their midst (Ezek. 2:5). If the watchman failed to sound the alarm, the blood was on his hands; but if he gave warning that went unheeded, he was absolved. The blood was not on his hands (Ezek. 3:17-19).

The most liberating experience for a minister is the discovery that he is not responsible for getting results; he is only responsible for doing what God tells him to do. His task, as with the Old Testament prophets, is to deliver the message given him by the Lord.[11] If the convicting power of the Holy Spirit cannot cause a person to submit to the Lord, all the gimmicks or psychological tricks of a preacher cannot bring about a genuine commitment.

Notes

1. The Hebrew word is "ark" in verse 18; but because the ark was supposed to be in Kiriath-jearim at this time (1 Sam. 7:2), the Septuagint substitutes the word "ephod." H. W. Hertzberg, *I and II Samuel* (Philadelphia: The Westminster Press, 1964), p. 114, cautions against discarding the traditional reading too hastily, however.

2. By definition a theophany is a visible manifestation of God. In the Bible theophanies may be through nature (a storm, a burning bush, a pillar of fire). They may be in human form (Gen. 18). The "angel of the Lord" is a theophany of God. Theophanic appearances of God are common in the Old Testament, but the New Testament theophany is limited to one—the incarnate Christ. God in human flesh was the climactic theophany of all revelation (Heb. 1:1-2).

3. James Barr, *Old and New in Interpretation* (New York: Harper & Row, Publishers, 1966), p. 22.

4. Willis Judson Beecher, *The Prophets and the Promise* (Grand Rapids: Baker Book House, 1905), p. 132.

5. Isaiah did make reference to disciples or "learners" (Isa. 8:16).

6. Though many have attempted to do so in a technical discipline called redaction criticism.

7. H. H. Rowley, ed., *The Old Testament and Modern Study* (London: Oxford University Press, 1951), p. 159.

8. Jeremiah 5:1-6; 13:1-11; 16:1-13; 18:1-12; 19:1-15; 25:15-29; 27—28; 32:1-15; 35:1-19; 51:59-64.

9. Ezekiel 3:26-27; 4:1-17; 5:1-17; 12:1-20; 21:18-23; 24:15-27; 37:15-23.

10. Other unnamed prophets would include Malachi, Isaiah 40—66, and Zechariah 9—14 on the lists of scholars who do not believe that these books or portions were written by the prophets whose names they bear. They rather feel that these Scriptures were authored by a later, unknown person.

11. Shortly before his crucifixion Jesus prayed to his Father: "I have brought you glory on earth by completing the work you gave me to do" (John 17:4, NIV). But even our Lord's earthly ministry would have been judged a failure

by the standards of his time. Many did not experience healing because of their unbelief. The Jewish leaders rejected him. There was jealousy among the disciples. One of the twelve was a traitor. Not everyone who heard him was saved. Therefore, how could he say that his work was finished? The answer is found in his own words: "I have revealed you to those whom you gave me out of the world. They were yours; you gave them to me and they have obeyed your word. Now they know that everything you have given me comes from you. *For I gave them the words you gave me* and they accepted them" (John 17:6-8a, NIV; italics were added by author). As was true of the Old Testament prophets, Jesus' task was to deliver the message given him by God, a message which for him included a cross.

4

"And it Will Come to Pass"
(Interpreting the Prophetic Message)

Some things can be said concerning the prophets upon which everyone would agree. They were courageous, sincere, devoted, self-sacrificing men of personal integrity. However, the most significant aspect of prophecy—how to interpret the message—is also the area in which there is the least agreement. At one extreme are those who believe that it is absolutely impossible for anyone to predict future events. Therefore, they insist that the prophets were speaking only to the people of their own times. Whatever fulfillment was intended by their words has already occurred. This is the historical school of interpretation.

At the other extreme are those who regard the prophets with almost mystical reverence and believe that their messages contain a blueprint for the coming ages. These exegetes prepare charts and chronologies of the course of future history, based on their understanding of what the prophets have said. For them the prophet was like a person with a crystal ball in his hand, gazing into the future. Their prophets appear not to have had any particular concern for their own time. Instead, they were preoccupied with what would happen hundreds of years in the yet uncharted future. This is the futuristic school of interpretation.

Even more unfortunate than the inability to agree on the interpretation of prophecy is the attitude that these two opposing schools of interpretation take toward each other. The historical school tends to look condescendingly upon the futuristic school, whereas the futuristic school suspects that the historical school does not believe the Bible.

Though it is not the purpose of this study to suggest a program of reconciliation for the two opposing schools, I do propose to set forth some guidelines which are reasonable for both to consider. They also will make the attainment of correct interpretation of prophecy more likely. In the paragraphs that follow, eleven guidelines are proposed. They have proved to be helpful to me in interpreting Old Testament prophecy.

The Prophet Had a Message for His Time

In order to arrive at a correct interpretation of prophecy, it is imperative to begin by asking, "What message did the prophet have for the people of his time? What was the historical situation that caused him to speak as he did?" It is incredible to suppose that the prophets were totally oblivious to the problems and crises of their own times. It is equally difficult to believe that God would have sent them to speak about matters that were irrelevant to their situation.

It does not seem likely that God would send Isaiah to Judah, when she was threatened by invasion from a coalition of Syria and Israel, to announce in effect, "I don't have anything to say about the threat against you people of Judah. However, don't be upset. God is going to send the Messiah in about seven hundred years!" (Isa. 7:14). What kind of comfort would that have been for a people faced with imminent death and destruction? Suppose for a moment that our world were on the brink of an atomic holocaust that would destroy civilization as we know it. Is it likely that God would send a prophet at such a time to say, "Don't worry. I'm going to let you in on a secret. The Lord is going to return in the year 2700"?

God cares for the present situation. He lives with us in the present. If he sent a prophet into our midst, it would be for the purpose of speaking to our situation and our concerns. Apply this principle to chapter 7 of Isaiah. When Isaiah said, "The virgin will be with child and will give birth to a son, and will call him Immanuel" (7:14, NIV), was he *only* announcing the Messiah who would not appear until almost seven hundred and thirty years later? Or did he have a message for the crisis that faced Judah in 735 BC?

When Isaiah 7:14 is read in the context of the entire chapter, it is clear that Isaiah was speaking a word of comfort for his nation, which was threatened with destruction. He was trying to assure them that in a very short time the threat would be ended if they would trust in God. He said that the crisis would last no longer than it would take for a young woman to marry, conceive, and have a child. The danger would end while that child was still quite young—two or three years old at the most.

On what basis, then, could the people of Judah be assured of deliverance? The sign of "Immanuel" was their assurance. Immanuel means "God with us." The sign meant that the assurance of God's presence with his people would be given through a name for a yet unborn child. It was not unknown to give a child a name that contained a message from God (see Hos. 1:4,6,9; Isa. 7:3; 8:3). How reassuring it is to know that God is concerned about any threats to his people and will take measures to protect those who trust in him.

I believe that this is the proper way to begin an interpretation of Isaiah 7:14. However, putting the prophecy in a historical context does not require that the meaning be exhausted in that one historical situation. Therefore, a second guideline for interpreting prophecy needs now to be considered.

Prophecy Is Dynamic

The statement that "prophecy is dynamic" describes a second and frequently denied characteristic of prophecy. True, the prophet did have a message for the people of his day; but the meaning was not always exhausted in that one situation. The genius of prophecy (and an evidence of its inspiration) is that the same prophetic word can be "fulfilled" on more than one occasion.

Consider Isaiah 6:9-10. The background of these words is found in the initial call of Isaiah. God was preparing him for a difficult ministry and for an indifferent response from the people of Judah. They would hear but not understand; their ears would be heavy, and they would shut their eyes to his warnings. In Matthew 13:14-15 Jesus quoted Isaiah 6:9-10 and said that the prophecy was "fulfilled." Jesus had been speaking to people who refused to hear him. Isaiah's words described just as accurately the people of Jesus' time as those to whom Isaiah spoke in his time.

But we are not through with this prophecy. In Acts 28:26-27 Paul quoted the same passage and said that it was being fulfilled again because "Some were convinced by what he said, but others would not believe" (Acts 28:24, NIV). Which interpretation is correct? Was it fulfilled in Isaiah's time, during Jesus' earthly ministry, or during Paul's missionary travels? If one grants the principle of dynamic fulfillment, then the answer is that the prophecy was equally fulfilled on all three occasions. And it is also being fulfilled today!

Consider another example of a dynamic prophecy. Placed in its historical setting and interpreted in the total context of the passage, Isaiah 49:6 says that God was going to make the nation Israel a light to the nations. In Luke 2:32 Simeon quoted Isaiah and said Jesus was that "light." Acts 13:47 quotes Isaiah again and says that witnessing Christians (such as Paul and Barnabas) were the light for the Gentiles. By extension, Christians today are still fulfilling the prophecy. Can all these interpretations be correct? The answer is yes, if one grants the validity of the dynamic principle of prophecy.

Return to the Isaiah 7:14 passage and apply the dynamic principle. Isaiah had a message for the people of his time, but it had a remarkably different fulfillment hundreds of years later. The greater fulfillment occurred at Bethlehem in a stable with the birth of our Lord (Matt. 1:23). In Bethlehem "Immanuel" ("God with us") took on a new dimension of meaning through the incarnation. By means of the birth, earthly life, and resurrection of Jesus, God is now with us in a way that even Isaiah did not fully anticipate.

The suggestion that even the prophet may not have understood the full significance of his own oracles requires a third guideline for the correct interpretation of prophecy.

The Prophet Did Not Understand All the Implications of His Message

Martin Buber, the best-known Jewish theologian of this century, said that the task of the prophet was to "announce a mystery, not to interpret it."[1] It was not required of him to explain all that his words might imply, and it is probable that even the prophet did not understand all that he was saying. Nor was it necessary for him to understand how it would eventually be fulfilled.

Some people visualize revelation to be like a giant movie screen dropped from heaven before the prophet as an audience of one. There he sat, watching future history unfold before his eyes! It is not necessary to insist that when Isaiah spoke the Immanuel prophecy (7:14), he had first been given a preview of the baby Jesus wrapped in swaddling clothes, lying in a manger, with the angels in the heavens singing "Glory to God" (Luke 2:1-14).

On the other hand, because we must never limit the sovereignty of God, we should not dogmatically say that such a complete revelation was impossible—that is, if we believe in revelation at all. There are passages in the New Testament which seem to indicate that the prophets were aware of profounder meanings contained in their messages (see John 11:49-52; 12:41; Acts 3:24; Rom. 1:2; 1 Pet. 1:10-12).

It does seem strange, however, that if any prophet did receive a clear, full-blown vision of the cross and the empty tomb, he would have kept such news to himself. At least there are no preserved messages of the prophets that suggest they had such insight. Also, it is clear that the Jews in New Testament times disagreed about what kind of person the Messiah would be. They seemed to be expecting an astute political and military leader who would free them from the yoke of Rome and would restore the grandeur of the days of David and Solomon. They rejected the idea of a poor, nonviolent Messiah who spoke of a kingdom in terms of moral and spiritual qualities.

The Old Testament prophets did not announce the messianic doctrine more clearly because they probably did not understand it fully themselves. The revelation given to each prophet was partial and incomplete. A cursory study of the Old Testament messianic passages makes it quite clear that no single prophet gave a complete messianic description.

Hebrews 1:1-2 reminds us that revelation to the prophets was partial. That is to say, God gave the revelation in small fragments to many men over a period of many centuries, "but when the time had fully come, God sent his Son" (Gal. 4:4, NIV).

This "fuller meaning" (*sensus plenior*) has been defined as "the deeper meaning, intended by God but not clearly intended by the human author, that is seen to exist in the words of Scripture when they are studied in the light of further revelation or of development in the understanding of revelation."[2]

A present-day illustration of this principle is found in the experience of the pastor who carefully prepares a sermon with a particular situation in mind (and sometimes with a particular person in mind!). He delivers it clearly and forcefully so that no one could have missed the point he was making. However, to his astonishment, while standing at the door greeting the departing parishioners, one of them says, "That sermon spoke to me." Upon further inquiry, the pastor may be chagrined to discover that the message "spoke" in a way that did not have the remotest connection with what he was saying. God can take his word and multiply it like the loaves and fishes, beyond all our expectations.

Some Prophecies Are Conditional

The reminder that some prophecies are conditional is an important guideline for correct interpretation of prophecy. If we forget that fact or ignore it, we may formulate all kinds of distorted notions about prophecy. Some prophecies are conditional, and the conditions may be stated or implied. When stated, the key word to look for is "if." "If you will obey, I will bless you; if you disobey, I will curse you" (author's paraphrase; see Deut. 11:27-28; compare Jer. 18:7-10).

Failure to appreciate the conditional nature of many of God's promises brought disaster to Israel. When God made a covenant with Israel at Mount Sinai, he promised them many blessings. With the passing of centuries the people became convinced that it did not matter how many of God's laws they broke. They were confident that he would continue to bless them in spite of their unfaithfulness. But his promises of blessing given at Mount Sinai were conditioned upon the obedience of the people.

Many people today are still interpreting the biblical promises to Israel as though they were unconditional. They believe that the Jewish people are returning to Israel today in fulfillment of Old Testament promises made by the prophets. There are, however, adherents of a literal return of the Jews to Israel *who do not believe the present return is that predicted by the Bible.* They point to Deuteronomy 30:1-6, which says that Israel will not be gathered from the nations and return to its land until *after* the people have returned to the Lord and obey him. Is it possible that the same error is being repeated today that was made in ancient Israel—the belief that God will bless his people by fulfilling all his promises to them in spite of their continued disobedience?

If the condition of the prophecy is stated but ignored, how

much more difficult it is to recognize those prophecies with implied conditions. A good example of an implied condition is found in the message of Jonah: "Yet forty days, and Nineveh shall be overthrown" (Jonah 3:4). Unless this message of judgment were conditional—that is, unless it allowed for the possibility of repentance and escape from destruction—how could we explain Jonah's reluctance to go to Nineveh in the first place? If he had understood the message to be an unconditional announcement of the doom of Nineveh, how would he have responded? He surely would have taken the next camel express (or whatever was the fastest means of transportation at the time!) to Nineveh to tell its inhabitants that they were going to be destroyed by God.

However, Jonah must have known there was a possibility, however remote, that Nineveh would repent and escape God's judgment. But he was unwilling to share his gracious, compassionate God (Jonah 4:2) with the hated Ninevites. If one insists that Jonah's message was unconditional, he must admit that a prophetic message given by God did not come true, for Nineveh was not destroyed forty days later.

Haggai 2:19 is another example of an implied condition. It simply says, "From this day on I will bless you." Haggai spoke these words after the returned exiles had started rebuilding the Temple in 520 BC. He had told them earlier that they did not have enough to eat, sufficient clothing to protect them from the cold, or adequate shelter because they had neglected the building of the Temple.

Haggai 2:19 could have been understood by the people to mean that with the work of rebuilding under way, they would no longer suffer any physical want. However, such was not the case. Life continued to be harsh and difficult in Judah. The prophecies of Malachi, delivered some sixty years later, make clear why God did not bless them materially when the Temple was rebuilt. They continued to be disobedient; therefore, he would not bless them, though he had told Haggai he would. The

Deuteronomic blessings and curses clearly were implied in the promise of Haggai 2:19. "Obey and you will be blessed; disobey and you will be cursed" (author's paraphrase; see Deut. 11:27-28).

Some Prophecies Are Messianic

It seems almost unnecessary to include as a guideline for correct interpretation of prophecy an affirmation that some Old Testament prophecies are messianic. How else could one explain the rise of the messianic hope in Israel apart from the prophets' contribution to this belief? From what other source could it have arisen? Whether one is talking about the Jewish or Christian concept of Messiah (and they are different), both find their origin in the messages of the Old Testament prophets.

Jesus walked along the Emmaus Road with two of his disciples after his resurrection, unrecognized by them. He rebuked them for having lost hope: "How foolish you are, and how slow of heart to believe all that the prophets have spoken! And beginning with Moses and all the Prophets, he explained to them what was said in all the Scriptures concerning himself" (Luke 24:25,27, NIV). This passage alone is sufficient warrant for a Bible student to turn to the Old Testament and to search for those Scriptures that can properly be called messianic.

It is unfortunate, however, that one of the Emmaus Road disciples could not record for posterity those Old Testament passages that Jesus said spoke about him! It would have spared a great deal of effort on the part of some to find Christ "hidden behind every verse." It is not likely, for example, that the messages of judgment which Amos delivered concerning the Philistines, Edomites, Ammonites, Moabites, and other nations surrounding Israel should be searched for hidden meaning. Amos was speaking messages of judgment to nations that existed historically at that time. He was not cryptically speaking of the Messiah (Amos 1:3 to 2:3).

It is just as erroneous to look for Christ in every verse of the

Old Testament as it is to deny the messianic content altogether. Some words of the prophets must be interpreted messianically in the light of the New Testament. For example, the relatively unknown book of Zechariah contains some of the most remarkably precise messianic predictions in the Old Testament (Zech. 9:9; 11:12; 12:10; 13:7; 14:4). However, not every verse in the Old Testament will yield a hidden reference to the Messiah, except through a most creative imagination.

There Is No One Method
for Interpreting All Prophecies

The preceding guideline implies that the New Testament takes Old Testament prophecies and claims that they have been fulfilled by Jesus of Nazareth as the long-awaited Messiah. I believe this is a legitimate way of relating the Old Testament to the New. Some scholars refer to this relationship as the principle of promise-fulfillment. In the Old Testament there is a forward look, a tension, a sense of incompleteness, which is only resolved in the New Testament.

However, having agreed that Old Testament prophecies are fulfilled in the New Testament does not resolve all the problems. Is there a consistent principle of interpretation followed by New Testament writers that can be discovered and applied to other Old Testament passages not specifically interpreted in the New Testament? If so, the key could be used to unlock the meaning of Old Testament predictions yet unfulfilled.

Some people think that they can turn any part of the Old Testament and unlock its hidden meaning because they believe they have discovered a key to prophecy. However, as proof that there is no such key or secret code, one only needs to study those Old Testament passages whose fulfillment is specifically given in the New Testament. No consistent key to New Testament fulfillment will be discovered.

There are, in the first place, some Old Testament passages that do not even appear to be predictive. Yet the New Testament reinterprets them and gives their fulfillment. For example, Isaiah 29:13 describes the unresponsive people in Isaiah's time. Seemingly, the verse is not predictive at all. Yet in Matthew 15:7-8 Jesus said that Isaiah was prophesying of the scribes and Pharisees who were confronting him at that moment. Hosea 11:1 is clearly a historical reference to the Exodus with no apparent predictive element in it. Yet Matthew 2:15 says that the flight of Jesus and his parents to Egypt during Herod's persecution and their later return was the fulfillment of Hosea's words. Isaiah 53:1 seems to be only a rhetorical question. However, John 12:38 says it was fulfilled by the refusal of the people to believe in Jesus, though he had performed many signs before them.

Even those Old Testament passages that unmistakably describe future events are given such unexpected interpretations in the New Testament that it is impossible to discover any exegetical principles that governed the New Testament writers' use of the Old Testament. For example, Amos 9:11 would probably have been understood by Amos' hearers as a promise of the restoration of the Davidic dynasty. Acts 15:16-18 says, however, that the responsiveness of the Gentiles to the preaching of Paul and Barnabas was the fulfillment of Amos' prophecy. Isaiah 7:14 predicted the resolution of a potentially dangerous military crisis within a short time. Yet Matthew 1:23 says it was fulfilled in the virgin birth of Jesus. Joel 2:28-32 describes the Day of the Lord in terms of fire and smoke, the darkening of the sun, and the turning of the moon to blood. A literal interpretation would anticipate unprecedented cosmic upheavals. However, Peter (and wasn't he inspired by the Spirit?) said that the words of Joel were fulfilled on the day of Pentecost by the strange behavior of the followers of Jesus as they received the Spirit (Acts 2:16-21).

Ezekiel 34:23, if interpreted literally, predicts that David will be resurrected and rule over his people. The New Testament transfers this promise to Jesus, a descendant of David.

Malachi 4:5 predicted the return of Elijah before the Day of the Lord,[3] but Jesus said that John the Baptist fulfilled the prophecy (Matt. 17:12; compare Matt. 11:14; Mark 9:11-13;

Luke 1:17). We do not understand Jesus to be saying that John was a reincarnation of Elijah. He was saying that in the spirit of Elijah, who appeared out of the wilderness to denounce the people's sins and to call them to repentance, John fulfilled the prophecy (compare also Isa. 40:3-5 with Luke 3:4-6). To compound the problem of the John the Baptist passages, John specifically denied that he was Elijah (John 1:21), though Jesus said he was. John did not understand that he was a fulfillment of Old Testament prophecy.

Other Old Testament passages could be cited of which the fulfillment is given in the New Testament (for example, Jer. 31:15; compare Matt. 2:17-18). However, it is impossible to discover in any of them a consistent principle or key that could be applied to other Old Testament passages to extract their meaning for the future.

This fact does not, however, deter many well-intentioned Christians from continuing to give all kinds of unusual interpretations to Old Testament prophecy. For example, Meshech of Ezekiel 38:3 is interpreted as Moscow; and Gomer of Ezekiel 38:6 becomes Germany because of slight similarities in spelling. The number of the beast, 666 (Rev. 13:18), has been a prime target through the centuries for those who think a code can be broken that will identify the beast. Positive identifications have been made of the beast as the emperor Nero, the pope, Napoleon, Hitler, Stalin, and even Henry Kissinger!

These exegetes claim to have discovered the key that enables them to turn to any part of the Old Testament and announce how it will be fulfilled. Bible students would do well to use caution in these areas of biblical interpretation.

Accept New Testament Interpretations, But Be Cautious About Interpreting Other Old Testament Passages

Some scholars will not accept New Testament interpretations of the Old Testament as valid. They say that this was the way people did it in New Testament times in their cultural context.

These scholars insist that ancient exegetical methods are not valid for us and that those interpretations are not necessarily correct.

Every person must, of course, establish his own principles of interpretation. For myself, I prefer to accept the New Testament interpretations of Old Testament prophecies because I believe that the New Testament writers were inspired. However, since there are no discernible principles or consistent ways in which the New Testament writers used the Old Testament, I am reluctant to assume that I can go to any other part of the Old Testament and find its hidden meaning. I am equally reluctant to describe the fulfillment of what appears to be still unfulfilled.

Sincerity or piety is not sufficient reason to justify the misuse to which some subject the Old Testament. It was noted earlier that some of the false prophets were sincere, though sincerely self-deceived. The most fertile field for this type of interpretation today is among those seeking for "signs of the times," even though the New Testament repeatedly tells us that we cannot know when the end will come.[4] Even the prophet Daniel did not understand his own visions as well as some modern exegetes claim they do (Dan. 8:27; 12:8)! When he asked the man clothed in linen how it would all end, he was told that the words were shut up and sealed until the time of the end (Dan. 12:9). We need to heed this biblical admonition.

When the New Testament does not clearly offer an interpretation, it is far better to keep silent than to say we know when we really do not know. Caution is the watchword in interpreting Old Testament prophecy.

Remember That the Bible Contains Figurative Language

Parts of the Bible are to be interpreted literally, but other parts are couched in figurative or symbolic language. If we give a symbolic or figurative interpretation to a statement that was intended to be literal, we will seriously distort the meaning. It is equally true that if we give a literal interpretation to a statement that was intended to be figurative or symbolic, we will seriously distort its meaning.

Much of the Old Testament should be interpreted literally. When we read that Michal became the wife of David (1 Sam. 18:27) or that Omri built the city of Samaria (1 Kings 16:24), these statements are to be taken literally. However, when we read that "the mountains skipped like rams, the hills like lambs" (Ps. 114:4), we know we are reading figurative language. When we read that the he-goat struck the ram and broke his two horns (Dan. 8:5-7), we know this is symbolic language. To interpret such passages literally would be grotesque and would cause us to miss the meaning completely.

The real problem is that it is not always easy to determine whether a passage is to be understood literally or figuratively. When Jesus said that Lazarus had fallen asleep, the disciples were relieved for a moment because they took his words literally. They did not understand that he was speaking figuratively of Lazarus' death (John 11:11-13). Amos' prediction that days are coming when the harvest will be so abundant that the plowman shall overtake the reaper and the hills will flow with wine (Amos 9:13) is understood by some as a literal prediction. Others insist that it is figurative language.

In a vision Ezekiel was shown Jerusalem being destroyed by supernatural beings (Ezek. 9:5-7) with fire hurled from heaven (Ezek. 10:2,6-7). A literal interpretation would insist that this was the way Jerusalem was destroyed, but we know that the city was destroyed by the Babylonian army. Therefore, Ezekiel's vision is to be interpreted symbolically as a warning of Jerusalem's impending destruction. Does Ezekiel's vision suggest that similiar descriptions of supernatural judgment in the book of Revelation should also be interpreted symbolically?

What about the promises in the Old Testament concerning Israel? Some Bible students say that every promise made to Israel that has not yet been fulfilled must be fulfilled literally in the future. Others say that the promises to Israel were nullified because of Israel's disobedience. Still others say that all the promises made to Israel have been fulfilled in the church, the spiritual seed of Abraham, the children of the promise (Rom. 9:6-8; see also John 8:42-44).

Who is right? If Elijah can be fulfilled in John the Baptist and David can be fulfilled in Jesus Christ, could not other passages that seem to require a literal fulfillment also be fulfilled symbolically? This is the kind of question about which a person who is honestly trying to understand the Scriptures should be open-minded. It reminds us that every Bible student should be slow to condemn those who differ with his interpretation of Scripture.

Because Prophecy Is Complex, Have an Attitude of Humility Toward It

The few examples of Old Testament prophecy which we have considered should be sufficient to reinforce the statement that prophecy is a complex phenomenon. No one has all the answers and should not pretend that he does. We do not lose face or credibility when we admit that we do not understand some things, do not have the answers for every question, and cannot see into the future. We need to recognize that there are mysteries remaining in the Scriptures.

Some people equate their interpretation of the Bible with believing the Bible itself. The inability to agree on interpretation has, of course, spawned many denominations. There is always a temptation for one denomination to brand all others as unbelievers. But if someone says to you, "I cannot accept your interpretation," it does not necessarily follow that he does not believe the Bible. The problem he has may be with your interpretation, not with the Bible. We must carefully preserve the distinction between believing the Bible and believing a particular interpretation of the Bible.

Several years ago a student gave me some carefully worked out charts to show that the then Secretary of State, Henry Kissinger, was the beast spoken of in Revelation 13:18. If I had told him that I did not believe his interpretation, he probably would have replied that I did not believe the Bible! A lot of name-calling and ugly accusations have resulted from the inability to separate belief in an interpretation of the Bible from belief in the Bible itself.

Lest the reader conclude that I am saying we can't be sure about anything in the Bible, let me add that there are certain nonnegotiables. If a person rejects the claims the Bible makes for itself, I would have to conclude that he does not believe the Bible. If he denies that Jesus is the Son of God, then a Christian will have to conclude that person is an unbeliever. However, if he does not believe that Meshech is Moscow (Ezek. 38:3) or that 666 is Henry Kissinger (Rev. 13:18), he has not denied the Bible. He has only said that he is unable to accept this kind of interpretation of the Bible.

Exercise a Responsible Attitude Toward Prophecy

Interpreting the Bible for others is an awesome responsibility. Whether the person doing so be one person explaining the Bible to another person, a teacher to a class, a preacher to a congregation, or a radio or television personality to the masses, an accounting will be required of each one (Matt. 12:36). Therefore, the task of explaining the Bible to others should not be undertaken lightly or flippantly.

The Bible should not be used as a kind of crystal ball to find out what is going to happen in the future at any given moment. To suggest that the prophets predicted the automobile (Nah. 2:4) or the airplane (Isa. 40:31) or Watergate (Neh. 8:1) is a blatant misuse of the Scriptures. This kind of "interpretation" can give all kinds of erroneous impressions about the function of Old Testament prophecy. To say that "USA" in the word Jerusalem proves that the United States of America is the new Jerusalem is irresponsible. To say that the Anglo-Saxons are the ten lost tribes of Israel because "Isaac's son" sounds a little bit like Saxon is indefensible. All such bizarre interpretations of the Old

Testament would be humorous except for the fact that many people take them seriously.

We should not constantly be using the Bible to discover the sensational, the hidden, and the bizarre. Such use of the Bible is irresponsible. It degrades the Word of God and will result in serious disillusionment on the part of trusting people when they discover that these are not legitimate ways of interpreting the Scriptures. They should, of course, become disillusioned with the interpreter, not the Bible; but they usually are not able to make the distinction.

The Bible is the Word of God. It contains the revelation of him and his will that he graciously gave through the centuries to many people at many different times. It merits our most serious, respectful use.

Depend upon the Holy Spirit

The preceding ten guidelines for correct interpretation of prophecy are valid. There remains, however, one other guideline, the most important of all. It is the necessity of dependence upon the Holy Spirit for correct interpretation of God's Word.

The rational scholar would reply, "Nonsense. We must depend on our intellect and technical expertise to interpret the Bible because it is literature composed by men. It should be subjected to the same critical disciplines as any other literature." At the other extreme is the almost mystical attitude that no technical or academic preparation will aid in the interpretation of the Bible. All one has to do is to offer a brief prayer, open his Bible, and begin reading. The understanding will automatically be given to him.

Most of those reading this book would be uncomfortable with either of these extremes. We believe that the better prepared a person is, the more likely he is to interpret the Scriptures correctly. Knowledge of original languages, grammar, syntax, historical background, cultural context, and literary forms will help produce a more accurate interpretation. But even with all the technical training and ability a Bible student may have, there is still a plus factor working for the person who believes in and depends upon the Spirit to teach what otherwise could never be fully understood (John 14:26; see also Gal. 1:12; Eph. 1:17; 1 John 4:6; Heb. 5:12).

There are other guidelines that could be added to the list, but the application of these eleven should help every Bible student achieve the goal of correctly handling the Word of truth (2 Tim. 2:15).

Notes

1. Martin Buber, *The Prophetic Faith* (New York: Harper & Row, Publishers, 1960), p. 230.

2. Raymond E. Brown, "Hermeneutics," in *The Jerome Biblical Commentary*, vol. 2, ed. R. E. Brown, J. A. Fitzmyer, and R. E. Murphy (Englewood Cliffs: Prentice-Hall, Inc., 1968), p. 616.

3. Orthodox Jews, believing in a yet "literal" fulfillment of the promise, still wait for Elijah. At the time of the Passover meal they set a cup for Elijah at the table and leave the front door ajar as an expression of their hope that "perhaps Elijah will return this year."

4. See Matthew 16:4; 24:36,42-44; 25:13; Mark 13:32; Luke 12:39-40; Acts 1:7; 1 Thessalonians 5:1-2; 2 Peter 3:10; Revelation 16:15.

5

"My Servants the Prophets"
(The Obedience of the Prophet)

The prophets are not easy to understand. Part of the problem is our separation in time from their cultural context. Archaeologists and historians have enabled us to know a great deal about the world in which they lived. Even with all this knowledge, however, we cannot really enter into their milieu and know what it was like to live in the ancient Near East in the first millennium BC.[1]

Another difficulty we have with understanding the prophets grows out of different thought patterns. Our cultural background has been largely influenced by Greek philosophical and aesthetic thought. The Hebrew people of biblical times did not produce great philosophers or artists. The prophets did not speculate about the existence of God; uncritically, they believed in him. Their mode of expression was direct, vigorous, and blunt by our standards. They did not try to describe God or draw pictures of what they had seen in visions. They were only concerned with proclaiming the messages they had received from him.

They were not concerned about salary, personal safety, or personal advancement. Whatever home and family life they enjoyed seemed to be of secondary importance. At least, they do not tell us much about their personal lives.

Obedience as the Key to Understanding the Prophets

We search for a key to understand the prophets, but the search often seems futile. They were far too complex to reduce to dimensions we can comfortably handle and analyze.

However, there is one thing the prophets shared in common. This common factor may be the most significant clue to understanding them. The one attribute they all shared was their great devotion to God. They were absolutely committed to him and his cause. Their lives were marked by personal faithfulness that sharply contrasted with the faithlessness of the rest of Israel. There seemed to be no personal sacrifice too great, no demand too staggering, and no task too demanding to deter the prophets from proclaiming the messages they received from God.

God called the prophet "my servant."[2] This is perhaps the title that best describes the absolute submission of the prophet to the will of God. The Hebrew language does not have different words for "servant" and "slave." The translation "servant" suggests in our cultural context a free, more independent relationship between two parties than the word "slave." However, in the ancient world those whom we call servants were slaves. They were either born in that condition or made slaves through conquest or financial necessity. The slave had no will of his own. His life and his time were at the disposal of his master. The slave knew one thing, and that was to obey his master. The word "slave," though a bit harsh for our ears, more accurately describes the relationship between God and "my servants the prophets."

It should not surprise us to discover that obedience is the one quality that characterized all the prophets, for obedience is a central emphasis throughout the Old Testament. It was not an injunction only for prophets. It was for all Israel, for God's relationship with his people was based on and conditioned by their obedience. In fact, the Old Testament can just about be summarized in the words: "Obey and you will be blessed. Disobey and you will be cursed" (author's paraphrase; Deut. 11:27-28; see also Deut. 28). The English word "obey" comes from two Latin words, *ob* and *audire*, "to hear." Biblical Hebrew does not have separate words that mean "hear" and "obey"; the same word was used to express both ideas. It implies what the prophets clearly understood—that when a person heard the voice of God, he knew that he must obey the words he heard. The prophet knew that hearing the word of God did not denote a passive receiving of words into his mind. It meant a total response of his being to the word and his identification with it (Jer. 15:16; Ezek. 2:3).

The prophet did not require psychological or philosophical explanations in order to understand the necessity of obedience. His thought processes were uncluttered, simple, and direct. When he heard God speak, he felt compelled to obey (Amos 3:8). His was an automatic response to authority that parents ideally like to see in their children.

The key to understanding the emphasis on obedience in the Old Testament is found in an established pedagogical principle: Obedience is a key factor to rapid learning. The child who refuses to obey the instructions of his parents and teachers never learns as rapidly as the one who listens carefully and then attempts to carry out these instructions.

As an illustration of this principle, recall the experience of being introduced to the multiplication tables as a child. There was no shortcut to learning them. Only by the laborious repetition of "two times two equals four, two times three equals six, etc." did we learn to multiply. But suppose a child would fold his arms defiantly upon being asked to learn the multiplication tables and say to his teacher, "I won't learn them!" That child would not likely become a great mathematician, to say the least!

This pedagogical principle may be a key to understanding why God insisted that Israel obey him. Israel was, so to speak, in a kindergarten stage of religious experience at Mount Sinai. Therefore, God dealt with them as children when he gave them laws that they had to obey in order to please him. Until they grew in comprehension through obedience, it was not possible to give them the fuller revelation of himself in Christ that would set them free (John 8:32). Unfortunately, the Israelites were not very rapid learners. Jeremiah 22:21 says, "This has been your practice from your youth,/That you have not obeyed My voice" (NASB).

The prophets knew that offering animal sacrifices was not the way to please God. Samuel said, "To obey is better than sacrifice" (1 Sam. 15:22). Hosea echoed a similar sentiment (Hos. 6:6). Isaiah told the people that God did not delight in their sacrifices because of their disobedience (Isa. 1:10-20). Micah exhorted the people that walking with God was better than thousands of rams or ten thousands of rivers of oil offered in sacrifice (Mic. 6:7-8). Through Amos, God said, "I hate, I reject your festivals,/Nor do I delight in your solemn assemblies./ Even though you offer up to Me burnt offerings and your grain offerings,/I will not accept them . . ./But let justice roll down like waters,/And righteousness like an ever-flowing stream" (Amos 5:21-22,24, NASB; see also 4:4-5).

The same appeal was made through the prophet Jeremiah: "Obey My voice and I will be your God"(Jer. 7:23, NASB). Malachi condemned the priests because their attitude toward the sacrificial system was wrong (Mal. 1:6 to 2:9).

To digress for a moment: The doctrine of obedience is emphasized in the New Testament as well as in the Old Testament. The fact that grace has taken the place of law does not mean that disobedience has replaced obedience. Jesus did not say that he came to abolish the law and the commands of God. He came to fill the law full of meaning (Matt. 5:17). He did not see his message as contradictory to the demand for the obedience required by the law (Mark 10:17-19). On one occasion he summarized all the requirements of obedience to the law in two simple commandments: Love God, and love your neighbor as yourself (Matt. 22:37,39). On another occasion he summarized all the Old Testament laws even more succinctly in one statement: "Therefore whatever you want others to do for you, do so for them; for this is the Law and the Prophets" (Matt. 7:12, NASB; compare Rom. 13:8).

One might respond to these appeals to obedience by saying that Christians are under the authority of the New Testament, not the Old. Therefore, the injunction to love, which is distinctively New Testament, has replaced the Old Testament emphasis on obedience. However, love was clearly linked to obedience by Jesus on a number of occasions. He said, "Whoever has my commands and obeys them, he is the one who loves me" (John 14:21, NIV). He added, "If anyone loves me, he will obey my teaching" (John 14:23, NIV). On another occasion he warned, "Not everyone who says to me, 'Lord, Lord,' will enter the kingdom of heaven, but only he who does the will of my Father who is in heaven" (Matt. 7:21, NIV). In other words, we do not demonstrate that we love the Lord by our words, however eloquent and beautiful they may be. We prove our love by our willingness to obey him. "For our love for God means that we obey his commands" (1 John 5:3, TEV). John added that obedience is an evidence of salvation (1 John 2:3-5).

In the Old Testament the lives of the prophets are models of the kind of obedience that God expected from his people. In the New Testament Jesus is our model of obedience. "And being found in appearance as a man, he humbled himself and became obedient to death—even death on a cross!" (Phil. 2:8, NIV; see also Heb. 5:8). It was his obedience that will make many righteous (Rom. 5:19).

God's demand for obedience obviously irked Israel (even as it does some Christians!), and she cast off his yoke like a wild animal (Hos. 4:16; 8:9; Jer. 2:24). By contrast, the prophets responded as did the psalmist: "I delight to do thy will, O my God" (Ps. 40:8).

Prophets as Examples of Obedience

We must not, however, paint an overly idealized picture of the prophets that would imply that they never had any problems with the will of God. Jeremiah perhaps had greater difficulty than any other prophet with submission to God's will. Or does it only appear that he had more difficulty because he tells us more about his struggles?

Ezekiel, by contrast, seemed so perfectly self-disciplined and obedient that there was nothing too difficult for God to ask him to do. He did not object when God asked him to shave off all his hair, even though ordinarily shaving the hair was reserved for an act of mourning, an expression of disgrace, or as a badge of enslavement (Ezek. 5:1-4). When told that his wife was about to die and that he must show no grief, Ezekiel obeyed without a word of protest, though he must have felt deep grief for his loss (Ezek. 24:15-18).

The only time this "man of iron" showed the slightest difficulty with carrying out God's commands involved what would seem to us a rather trivial matter involving the ritual laws of cleanness. God asked him to cook food over human dung. To do so would have made him ceremonially unclean. When Ezekiel objected, God allowed him to substitute animal dung (Ezek. 4:9-15).

If our interpretation of the third chapter of Hosea is correct,[3] the prophet Hosea serves as another example of an obedient prophet. The prophet's wife, Gomer, deserted her husband and children to serve as a temple prostitute in the Baal fertility rituals. Later, having lost her beauty and her usefulness, she was sold as a slave to pay the debts she had accumulated. God told Hosea to go down to the slave market and buy his wife out of bondage, to restore her to their home and his heart. How difficult this must have been for a man whose love and trust had been betrayed by a faithless wife bent on the pursuit of her own pleasures. Yet Hosea obeyed God.

A third example of an obedient prophet is Daniel. Though he is not included in the Jewish Bible among the prophets,[4] he has come to be thought of as one of them, particularly because of his visions regarding future events. From his youth Daniel's chief desire was to obey God. He was unwilling to eat the rich foods served him from the table of King Nebuchadnezzar, though by refusing to do so he risked incurring the wrath of the king (Dan. 1). He could have reasoned that it was all right to break the dietary laws he had so carefully observed from his childhood because he was an exile in a foreign land. Furthermore, he was separated from home and the pressures of family influence and religious traditions.

How easy it would have been for him and the other young men carried into exile with him to conclude that breaking the dietary laws was justifiable. Daniel would know other occasions when his obedience to God would threaten his life (Dan. 6).

The Bible mentions unnamed prophets who were put to death by their own people. Though details of their deaths are not given, it is a safe assumption that they lost their lives because they chose to obey God rather than to please the people.[5]

Symbolic Acts as Expressions of Obedience

The prophets demonstrated their obedience to God in many ways. One of the most unusual expressions of their obedience is found in the so-called symbolic acts which they performed. These are sometimes referred to as enacted parables (see chap. 4). The symbolic act was a mode of revelation particularly associated with Jeremiah and Ezekiel. God would speak to the prophet and instruct him to perform a certain deed. The significance, however, lay not in the act itself but in the message it symbolized.

These symbolic acts frequently caused the prophet great personal inconvenience. For example, Jeremiah traveled to the Euphrates River to bury and later to dig up a garment. A total of about 1,500 miles for the two trips was involved (Jer. 13:1-7).[6]

Sometimes these acts brought embarrassment to the prophet. For example, Ezekiel was required to shave off his hair (Ezek.

5:1-4), a humiliating act because a man's hair was his crowning glory.

Sometimes the symbolic act brought personal grief to the prophet. For example, Ezekiel was told that his wife was going to die (Ezek. 24:15-18). The entire marriage experience of Hosea may be interpreted as a symbolic act, for in growing out of his own personal marital tragedy, he learned how deeply Israel had grieved God. He also learned the dimensions of God's love—that is, willing to forgive in spite of gross unfaithfulness.

Some of the acts performed by the prophets probably subjected them to ridicule and possibly even to the charge that they were deranged. For example, Isaiah went naked for three years (Isa. 20:2-3). Ezekiel dug a hole through the wall of his house and crawled out through it at night (Ezek. 12:1-7). This same prophet constructed a miniature replica of Jerusalem and "played war" (Ezek. 4:1-3). Jeremiah went about the city wearing an ox's yoke on his back (Jer. 27:1-2). What would a church today say about its pastor who might do similar things?

Occasionally the symbolic act was a real test of the prophet's own faith in God. During the siege of Jerusalem by Nebuchadnezzar's army, real-estate values in Judah must have reached an all-time low. But during the siege, God told Jeremiah to pay the money for a piece of land that a kinsman of his wanted to sell (Jer. 32:1-15). The purchase would symbolize faith on the part of Jeremiah that the crisis would end one day and life would return to normal in Judah. We would call it a challenge to "put your money where your mouth is."

A severe test of obedience was put upon Jeremiah when God told him not to marry (Jer. 16:1-2). In any age, if it were not the individual's own choice, the single life could be very difficult. It entails loneliness and separation from the normal satisfactions found in home and family life. In ancient Israel, however, the single life was even more difficult because it was expected that men would marry. The Talmud pronounces a curse on the man who was not married by age twenty! Marriage and children were looked upon as blessings from God. In the popular mind, to be deprived of home and family was interpreted as a sign of God's disfavor. When Job lost his children, his friends were sure that he had committed some terrible sin (Job 4:7; 11:6; 22:5).

A word of clarification may be in order concerning the nature of the symbolic acts, especially since it was stated earlier that some scholars refer to them as enacted parables. They were not narrated parables but were acts actually performed by the prophet. Their true significance, however, lay in the message contained in the act. The deed itself was a kind of "miniature" of what was actually going to happen in Israel.

For example, when Jeremiah smashed a clay bottle, his action symbolized the destruction of Jerusalem (Jer. 19:1-13). We are to understand that Ezekiel actually shaved off his hair and that his wife really died. Hosea actually experienced marriage with a woman who abandoned her family for a life of harlotry. The experiences were real, but they were used to communicate messages from God to his people.

Symbolic acts were also performed by pagan prophets, but for a different purpose. The neighbors of Israel believed that these symbolic acts contained magical power to bring about the larger deed they symbolized. Parallel to this ancient belief is the voodoo practice of sticking a pin in a doll in the belief that the person the doll represents will experience pain or even death. However, it should be made clear that the prophets of Israel did not share the superstitious beliefs of their pagan neighbors when they performed symbolic acts. They used them only as attention-getting vehicles for communicating messages from God to the people, and they always gave the interpretation of the symbolic act.

Conclusion

Many other illustrations could be given of the obedience of the prophets, but the lesson is clear. Perhaps the most impressive of all the qualities of the prophets was their unwavering obedience to God. Human logic says that to submit as completely to someone else as they did would be degrading; it would result in the loss of personal liberty and self-fulfillment.

However, across the pages of the Old Testament, the prophets emerge as persons who found true liberty. They realized their highest potential and greatest usefulness through obedience. Israel was enslaved by its worship of Baal and could not cast off the yoke (Jer. 18:12; see also 2:25). Their "pursuit of freedom" brought them only "swearing, deception, murder, stealing, and adultery . . . violence, so that bloodshed follows bloodshed" (Hos. 4:2, NASB).

Hosea predicted that, like the prodigal son of the New Testament (Luke 15:11-32), Israel would wake up some day and realize that her so-called freedom had not brought satisfaction. Then she would say, "I will go back to my first husband,/For it was better for me then than now!" (Hos. 2:7, NASB).

Judah's tragedy was that when she did wake up and call on God, it was too late. God had warned that the time would come when even if men as righteous as Noah, Daniel, and Job were in Jerusalem, they would be unable to save the city at the time of its destruction (Ezek. 14:14). Disobedience to God has a price tag on it that will be exacted at painful cost. Sometimes it is too late to repent (see Num. 14:39-45).

The "angry young man" and the rebel against all authority, even the authority of God, never really find happiness. The apostle Paul explained that there is no such thing as the totally free person. He said that we all have a master. We may choose sin as our master, but this choice will result in death. Or we may choose obedience to God and become servants of righteousness and thereby be freed from sin (Rom. 6:14-18).

It is one of the paradoxes of the Christian faith that the person who accepts the invitation of Jesus Christ to take his yoke upon himself discovers it to be easy and light (Matt. 11:28-30). We become truly free for the first time when we submit to the lordship of Christ (John 8:32,26).

Obedience to God is not a burden to be endured. It is actually the most positive expression of our confidence in him. On the human plane, if we do something that another person asks us to do, we are expressing confidence in that person. We do what he asks because we believe that whatever he asks us to do is good and is for our well-being. We trust him not to ask us to do anything that would harm us or is not in our best interest.

A never-forgotten incident from our own family convinced me that obedience is based on confidence. When our son was four, no amount of coaxing would persuade him to eat spinach. We used all the usual arguments—it tasted good and was good for him. We used what was supposed to be the clincher at that time—Popeye liked spinach! But nothing worked. He would not even taste the green stuff.

This impasse continued until one day his sister, seven years older, accomplished what all our pleading and coaxing had failed to do. She said, "David, I like spinach," and proceeded to eat hers with gusto. David looked at his sister and then at the spinach on his plate. Then, without a word, he began eating his spinach!

His sudden change can only be understood in light of the "love-worship" relationship that he enjoyed with his older sisters while growing up. They never tricked him or teased him, so he trusted them completely. His own suspicions of spinach were overcome because he had complete confidence in his sister. He knew from experience that she would not trick him or do anything to hurt him.

The application in respect to our willingness to do what God asks us to do is obvious. When we refuse to obey, whether the person be parent, teacher, friend, or God himself, we are saying that we really do not have confidence in him. The prophets believed in God. They had confidence that what he asked them to do was the best course of action to follow, both for them and for the nation.

A Christian mystic of another century said, "Perfect obedience would be perfect happiness if only we had perfect confidence in the power we were obeying."[7] The Old Testament prophets came as near as anyone ever has, other than our Lord himself, to this goal of perfect obedience.

Notes

1. The eminent historian R. G. Collingwood would disagree with this statement. He believed that it was possible to enter into the mind and thought processes of a person of another era and know what that person felt or thought. He said, for example, that a person can enter into the mind of Caesar and know what he was thinking. See Collingwood, *The Idea of History* (London: Oxford University Press, 1946; paperback reprint, 1972), pp. 213-217.

2. Numbers 12:7; 2 Kings 9:7,36; Isaiah 20:3; Jeremiah 7:25; Ezekiel 38:17; Daniel 9:17; Amos 3:7; Zechariah 1:6. Even the Babylonian ruler Nebuchadnezzar could be called a servant of God (Jer. 25:9; 27:6; 43:10) because he was an unwitting agent of the divine will. Cyrus, king of Persia, was called "my shepherd" (Isa. 44:28); in that context the term is the equivalent of a "servant."

3. Chapter 3 is a continuation of the prophet's marital experiences that begin in chapter 1. Any other interpretation destroys the obvious parallel with faithless Israel and God's desire to restore her.

4. Daniel is in the third division of the Hebrew Bible, the Ketubim ("Writings").

5. See, for example, 1 Kings 18:13; 2 Kings 9:7; 1 Chronicles 16:22; Jeremiah 2:30; Lamentations 2:20; Matthew 23:37.

6. Some scholars have identified the river as the nearby Perath (Jer. 13:5, NEB) or the town of Parah (Josh. 18:23) rather than the Euphrates because of the similarity of the spelling. It is true that the same purpose could have been accomplished at the nearby river, but it is not impossible that the more distant river was Jeremiah's actual destination. The longer journey would have made a deeper impression on the people. Also, life did not have the quality of "hurry" that characterizes twentieth-century living. Spending several months in foot travel would not have bothered Jeremiah.

7. Hannah Whitall Smith, *The Christian's Secret of a Happy Life* (Westwood, New Jersey: Fleming H. Revell Company, 1870—reprinted 1952 and 1968), p. 208.

6

"Son of Man"

(The Humanity of the Prophet)

The proper place to begin a study of one of the Old Testament prophetic books is with a study of the prophet himself. Learn all that can be known about the prophet as a person (where he lived, his family, his age, his occupation, his personality, etc.). Study the historical background to know what was going on in the world about him. Find out about the political, economic, social, and religious conditions in Israel in his day. Whatever can be known about the prophet helps immensely in understanding what he said and why he said it.

In addition to giving help in understanding the messages of the prophets, this kind of background study enables us to bring the prophet into focus as a human being. It is very easy to be in such awe of these men who stood against the whole nation, and we may forget they were flesh-and-blood human beings. They seemed forever fearless, hurling their messages of warning and denunciation without regard for personal consequences. We frequently depict the prophets, if not in shining armor, at least in glistening robes and projecting an aura of light about them, with fire in their eyes and thunder in their voices.

However, it is a mistake to think of the prophets as super-human, almost semidivine beings. The prophets felt pain and grief; they experienced loneliness and fear; they became discouraged and sometimes wanted to quit. They longed for acceptance among their people and an occasional word of gratitude. They could become angry, and they could weep. They had feelings and could be deeply hurt by the slanderous words people spoke behind their backs. They could be obedient to the will of God, but sometimes they rebelled against him. They were humble, with little regard for what people thought about them; but they could also be defensive and sometimes a little bit self-righteous. In short, they experienced all the emotions and personal conflicts involved in doing God's will that anyone else would experience.

In the following pages we will examine some of the prophets with a view to discovering those qualities and experiences which unmistakably reveal their true humanity.

Moses

Of all the Old Testament figures, Moses emerges in popular thought as the most majestic and nearly superhuman of all the prophets.[1] He is best remembered for his role in the heroic task of leading the Israelites out of slavery in Egypt. He was equal to every crisis they encountered in their journey and brought them to the Promised Land.

It is easy to lose sight of the human Moses, born to a slave family but raised in the royal court of Pharaoh. In a fit of anger he murdered an Egyptian (Ex. 2:12) and had to flee for his life. This same man made all kinds of excuses to escape the call God extended to him at Mount Sinai (Ex. 3:1 to 4:13). There is also a suggestion that his marriage was not ideal. On one occasion his wife bitterly denounced him (Ex. 4:25). As a result of her harsh words to him, he apparently sent her back to stay with her father for a time (Ex. 18:2). Neither his brother or his sister seemed to be pleased with his marriage (Num. 12:1-2).

The same Moses who could rise to heights of greatness as he pleaded with God not to destroy the Israelites could become infuriated with them. His fit of rage occurred just after telling God not to be angry with them (Ex. 32:11-14)! He smashed the stones on which the Ten Commandments had been written by the finger of God and ordered a slaughter of his own people (Ex. 32:19, 25-28).

Moses, who was patient and longsuffering with the Israelites on so many occasions, one day apparently had enough of their complaints. They were grumbling because of lack of water. God was willing to provide the water, but Moses had reached the breaking point. He smashed his staff against the rock that had been designated by the Lord as the source of water, instead of only speaking to the rock as he had been commanded. By means of this violent gesture he gave vent to his feelings about rebellious Israel. At the same time he may have wanted to smash a few heads the same way! As a result of Moses' loss of self-control, God said that his sin was so serious that he would not be allowed to enter the Promised Land (Num. 20:1-12).

The greatest figure in the Old Testament, who stood before God on Sinai until his face glistened with heavenly light, also had a temper that was difficult for him to control and patience that did have limits.

Samuel

Samuel is another of the great prophets of the Old Testament. His personal faithfulness from childhood to old age is impressive. He courageously delivered God's messages, whether to the priest Eli (1 Sam. 3:18), to King Saul (1 Sam. 15:26,28), or to the people of Israel (1 Sam. 12:1-18).

On one occasion he called the people together and asked them to accuse him of any wrongs he might have committed against them during the long years of his leadership. Not one charge was made against him (1 Sam. 12:4). Truly this was a remarkable record and one that set Samuel apart from ordinary mortals.

However, there are a few personal glimpses into the inner recesses of Samuel's life that humanize this otherwise austere and unblemished figure. His family life is shrouded in silence. More is known about his parents and his early childhood than about all his adult life, including his marriage. His wife is never mentioned, and we would not even know that he was married except for the mention of his sons.

It is the reference to the sons that gives a clue to one failing of Samuel. When Samuel was old, he appointed his own sons as judges over Israel (1 Sam. 8:1). His personal selection of judges to succeed him was in violation of the way previous judges had been chosen. Earlier judges were charismatic leaders who had been chosen by God. There was no established custom of hereditary succession. Samuel's choice of his sons could be excused, however, except that the young men were obviously not fit to lead Israel. They had "turned aside after dishonest gain and took bribes and perverted justice" (1 Sam. 8:3, NASB). This is a failing of leaders not limited to modern politicians! They were not at all like their father, and the people of Israel refused to accept them as Samuel's successors (1 Sam. 8:5).

Expository commentators usually make a great issue of the failure of the priest Eli to raise godly sons (1 Sam. 2:12,17,29). However, they rarely take note that Samuel was the same kind of father. Was Samuel too involved in the affairs of Israel to discipline his own sons? Was he an overindulgent father, who was blind to the wrongdoings of his sons? We must not be too hard on Samuel in the absence of all the facts about his homelife. However we explain them, it is clear that this great man of God had family problems just as do other people.

We also detect a sensitivity and defensiveness on the part of Samuel when the people refused to accept his sons as judges. "The thing displeased Samuel when they said, 'Give us a king to govern us' " (1 Sam. 8:6, RSV). It is true that their rejection of Samuel was in reality a rejection of God (1 Sam. 8:7). But would they have rebelled against Samuel if he had not tried to name his sons as his successors?

Another incident in Samuel's life serves to remind us that prophets were not omniscient like God. The Lord sent Samuel to Jesse to anoint a successor to Saul from among Jesse's sons. Samuel obviously did not have an "inside track" on which son would be named. As a matter of fact, he looked at the first son who was brought in and immediately said, "Surely the LORD's anointed is before Him" (1 Sam. 16:6, NASB).

However, with the rejection of the last of Jesse's seven sons, Samuel, puzzled and in confusion, asked Jesse if there might be another son. It was only then that the family remembered David, the youngest, whom they had not even bothered to bring into the house for consideration.

Samuel is usually characterized as a man of unimpeachable and flawless character. He does emerge, however, upon closer examination, as a human being, particularly with respect to the problem with his children and his sensitivity to criticism. His anointing of Saul's successor also reveals that prophets were not omniscient.

Elijah

The name Elijah invokes the image of a courageous prophet. He was the man who defied all the prophets of Baal in a remarkable contest on Mount Carmel to determine who was really God. He called fire down from heaven to consume his sacrifice and thereby convinced the Israelites that they should serve the Lord (1 Kings 18). He was also the prophet who accused King Ahab to his face of his wickedness in the affair of Naboth's vineyard (1 Kings 21:17-24). His rather remarkable removal from this world in a whirlwind at the end of his days on earth could easily have established this prophet as a supernatural being in the eyes of Israel (2 Kings 2:11).

Only one experience that we know about in the life of this great prophet mars the otherwise unblemished image of a man who might have become a mythological hero in later Jewish tradition. That experience was his reaction to the threats made against him by Queen Jezebel. The occasion was immediately after his greatest victory—the extermination of the prophets of Baal on Mount Carmel. When Jezebel learned what Elijah had done, she determined to have him killed before another day passed.

For a man who could call down fire from heaven, a threat

from Jezebel should have been dismissed as lightly as a cow brushing off a fly with a swish of its tail. But the unexpected reaction of the prophet upon learning of the threat against him was to run for his life to Beersheba (1 Kings 19:1-3)! A glance at a map will show that Beersheba was far to the south of Mount Carmel, not just a few miles away. Elijah's overreaction is paralleled by Jonah's flight to Tarshish to avoid going to Nineveh.

At the conclusion of his flight, Elijah sat down under a broom tree (1 Kings 19:5; "juniper tree," KJV). He was so despondent that he asked the Lord to take his life. Then he continued on to Mount Horeb where he poured out his complaints to the Lord. When the Lord asked him why he had gone all the way to Horeb, he petulantly replied that he had been zealous for the Lord's work, but all it had gotten him was an attempt on his life. In his self-pity he informed God that he was the only person on earth who was still faithful (1 Kings 19:8-14). God had to reassure the distraught prophet that there were seven thousand others who were still faithful. He added that there was work for the prophet to do (1 Kings 19:15-18).

If this one episode in the life of Elijah had not been preserved, it would be very difficult to discover the human Elijah. Clearly, however, the great man was human. Like some of us, he did not feel that his faithfulness had been properly noticed or rewarded by God. His life also reminds us that discouragement can follow quickly on the heels of a spiritual victory.

Elisha

Every person has his own threshold of sensitivity overload. Some people are offended easily, and others are hardly ever offended. The great prophet Elisha was extremely sensitive about his bald head! This is the prophet who pleaded for a double portion of the Spirit (2 Kings 2:9) and performed more recorded miracles than any other prophet (2 Kings 2—6). Yet he was so angry with some boys who mocked him one day saying, "Go up, you baldhead! Go up, you baldhead!" that he cursed them in the name of the Lord (2 Kings 2:23-24). Two bears came out of the woods and "tore"[2] forty-two of the boys. Whether the prophet's bald head was the result of natural baldness or a distinctive tonsure affected by holy men remains in dispute. But the point is clear: Elisha was extremely sensitive about his appearance!

Jonah

It would not be amiss to describe Elijah as a pouting prophet when he reminded God that he was the only faithful one left (1 Kings 19:14). There is another prophet who could also bear the label of the pouting prophet, and he is Jonah. By contrast with Elijah, who gives little evidence of being "tempted like in all points as we are," Jonah appears as the completely human prophet from the beginning to the end of the book that bears his name.

When God called him to go to Nineveh, he defiantly took a boat headed in the opposite direction to Tarshish.[3] Once in the boat he fell fast asleep, comforted in the belief that he had escaped God. Even when confronted with proof that he had not escaped God—the storm at sea and the lot cast by the sailors that fell upon Jonah—he still was unwilling to yield. He told the sailors to throw him overboard in order for the storm to cease.

His request should not be construed as an expression of unselfish concern for the lives of the sailors. It was a defiant gesture to God that meant: "I had rather be dead than go to Nineveh." It took a few days in the stomach of a fish to convince the reluctant prophet that he should go to Nineveh. However, he did not deliver his message with a great deal of enthusiasm. He preached to Nineveh only out of divine compulsion that there was nothing else he could do.

When Nineveh repented and was spared, Jonah should have been the happiest person in the world, but instead he was angry.

It seems unbelievable that, having been responsible for the greatest revival the world has ever known, Jonah could be unhappy with the results. What preacher today would not be walking on pink clouds if he preached a revival that resulted in one hundred conversions (or even ten)? Half a million Ninevites turned to God under the preaching of Jonah, but it brought him no joy.

Jonah went outside the city and sat down as though waiting to see if God would come to his senses and go ahead and destroy the city. God tried to reason with Jonah and to justify his treatment of Nineveh. But like a pouting child, the prophet still insisted that he would rather be dead than to continue living in a world governed by such a softhearted God.

We do not know whether Jonah repented of his attitude toward Nineveh because the book ends without telling us whether he was ever reconciled to a God who could forgive Ninevites.

From first to last Jonah was a rebel against the will of God. The recorded experiences of Jonah make no attempt to polish up the rather tarnished image of this rebellious and very human prophet.

Jeremiah

Most people discover that, of all the prophets, they identify most readily with Jeremiah. There is a kind of empathy that quickly develops between the reader and the "weeping prophet"[4] that is not felt with any other prophet. As we read those parts of the book where the prophet bares his soul,[5] we find ourselves saying time and again, "I have experienced similar feelings." We may say, "I have had similar moments of doubt and despondency" or, simply, "I understand what you are experiencing, Jeremiah."

A modern psychologist would probably analyze Jeremiah as a person with an inferiority complex who was preaching condemnation to others. To borrow the language of a recent best-seller, he would say that Jeremiah was preaching, "I'm not OK; you're not OK." From his inital call and for a number of years afterward, Jeremiah did not have a great deal of confidence in himself. He said, "Alas, Lord GOD!/Behold, I do not know how to speak,/Because I am a youth" (Jer. 1:6, NASB).

When he heard of a plot against his life, he did not piously pray, "Lord, forgive them for they know not what they do." His prayer was much more human: "Let me see thy vengeance on them" (Jer. 11:20). On another occasion he was disturbed by the same question that has troubled many people: "Why does the way of the wicked prosper?" (12:1). He contrasted his faithfulness to their hypocrisy and once again demanded that they get their just deserts: "Pull them out like sheep for the slaughter" (12:3). The reader seems to detect a note of self-righteousness in 12:3.

God's response seemed to be, "Jeremiah, you haven't seen anything yet. If you can't stand up to these petty trials, what will you do when the situation really becomes serious? Cheer up! The worst is yet to come!" (author's paraphrase of 12:5).

On another occasion in what appears to be a plaintive wail of self-pity, Jeremiah bemoaned his birth. He said that, though he had done no wrong, he had become a source of contention and everyone was cursing him (15:10). His depression so overwhelmed him that he complained that God had cut him off from all human friendships (15:17). He added that God was undependable "like a deceptive stream/With water that is unreliable" (15:18, NASB). He was referring to the mountain streams or *wadis* in Palestine that overflow with water from melting snows or rain in early spring. However, those same streams are completely dried up in the heat of summer when they would be most needed and appreciated.

As a reminder that even a prophet may overstep the bounds of propriety, God made it clear that such blasphemous words were about to cost Jeremiah the privilege of being a prophet. He rebuked Jeremiah, saying, "If you return, then I will restore you" and "You will become My spokesman" (15:19, NASB). God concluded by reminding Jeremiah that the task of the prophet was to lead the people to become like him by his words and example. He was not to become like them (15:19).

Jeremiah preached words of warning and impending judgment for forty years before Jerusalem was finally destroyed. It is understandable that the people would begin to react after a number of years of hearing the same gloomy words that never came true. They began to taunt Jeremiah when they met him on the streets: "Where is the word of the Lord? Let it come!" (17:15). Jeremiah finally reacted to his tormentors just as most of us would. He called on God for vengeance: "Let those who persecute me be put to shame, . . . Bring on them a day of disaster,/And crush them with twofold destruction!" (17:18, NASB). Though we cannot condone Jeremiah's harsh words, we can understand them.

At a later period in his ministry the people cast off all restraints and tried to put Jeremiah to death (38:4-6). Earlier they had attacked him by spreading rumors to destroy his reputation (18:18). When Jeremiah learned about the things being said behind his back, he told God to listen to the slanderous remarks. He reminded God how faithfully he had interceded for Judah in the past, but now his patience had been tested beyond human endurance. In a venomous outburst that we do not usually associate with this gentle, compassionate man, Jeremiah appealed to God:

"Therefore, give their children over to famine,/And deliver them up to the power of the sword;/And let their wives become childless and widowed./Let their men also be smitten to death,/Their young men struck down by the sword in battle . . ./Do not forgive their iniquity/Or blot out their sin from Thy sight./But may they be overthrown before Thee;/Deal with them in the time of Thine anger!"(Jer. 18:21,23, NASB).

Jeremiah's words were profoundly natural, but they were profoundly wrong; and we cannot justify them. However, they do remind us that when we continue to hurt other people and to malign them, they may reach a breaking point. "All scripture is

inspired by God" (2 Tim. 3:16), but all words recorded in the
Scriptures are not inspired by God. Satan speaks, and the words
of wicked men are also recorded. When Jeremiah in effect asked
God to "throw the book" at his enemies, we could not use his
words as proof-texts to justify similar attitudes. This is the man
Jeremiah speaking on his own initiative, not as the prophet of
God. His words serve to remind us that any servant of God can
on occasion act or speak contrary to God's desire.

Jeremiah was not the only prophet to suffer physical abuse as a
reward for proclaiming the word of the Lord, but he told us
more about his reaction to such mistreatment than anyone else.
The priest Pashhur heard Jeremiah prophesying and had him
beaten, put in stocks, and made a public spectacle (20:1-2). We
can imagine the prophet's humiliation as people came by and
ridiculed him and spat in his face. As soon as Pashhur released
him, Jeremiah cursed him and told the priest that he would be
taken as a captive to Babylon where he would die and be buried
(20:3-6).

Having taken care of Pashhur, Jeremiah then turned on God.
He began what could have become a final renunciation of his
prophetic ministry: "O Lord, Thou hast deceived me/and I was
deceived" (20:7). The word translated "deceived" is the same
word found in Exodus 22:16 to describe a young man seducing a
maiden. These are shocking words from the lips of a prophet!

Jeremiah was tormented by the realization that, even when he
determined never to speak another word in the name of the
Lord, he could not contain himself. The word was "like a burning fire/Shut up in my bones;/And I am weary of holding it in"
(20:9, NASB; see also 5:14; 6:11). The distraught man found
that he was miserable if he spoke God's word, and he was miserable if he did not speak.

For a moment, however, he seemed to take fresh courage. He
reassured himself that God was with him like a "dread cham-
pion" (20:11, NASB; "strong and ruthless," NEB). But his
resurging confidence evaporated almost as quickly as it ap-

peared, and he found himself wallowing in despair: "Cursed be the day when I was born; Why did I ever come forth from the womb/To look on trouble and sorrow,/So that my days have been spent in shame?" (20:14,18, NASB). There is no recorded response from God to these words. We believe, however, that even as we can sympathize with the prophet in such a moment, God grieved for his servant and brought reassurance to him.

It would be unfair to Jeremiah to close our observations about him after having concentrated only on those experiences that reveal his weakest moments. His testings must have eventually prepared him for the critical years of the siege and fall of Jerusalem. God had told him at the beginning of his ministry that he would make him a "fortified city, iron pillar and bronze walls, against the whole land" (1:18). The purging and refining that resulted from his testings brought him to the place where he did not whimper or flinch when his enemies prevailed upon the king to put him in a cistern to die (38:6).

When King Zedekiah demanded that Jeremiah not keep back a single word he had received from the Lord, the prophet courageously said, "Why should I tell you? You will only put me to death; and besides, if I gave you advice, you wouldn't listen to me" (author's paraphrase of 38:15). When Jerusalem fell to the victorious Babylonians in 587 BC, Jeremiah resisted the tempting offer tendered by Nebuchadnezzar to take up residence in Babylon where he could have lived in honor and comfort the rest of his life (39:11-12; 40:4-5). Instead, he chose to remain with the remnant of his defeated people to help the new governor, Gedaliah, in the difficult task of holding together what was left of the nation.

After the murder of Gedaliah, the people turned to Jeremiah for advice and agreed to do whatever he told them (42:2-3). He had learned long before that his words would not necessarily please them. If the choice was between telling them things that would please them and make him popular or giving them God's words, he had only one choice. So after praying ten days for guidance, he told the people that they must not flee to Egypt or be afraid of Nebuchadnezzar (42:7-12). For forty years before the fall of Jerusalem the people had not listened to Jeremiah. Therefore, it probably came as no surprise to him when they rejected his advice and fled to Egypt, forcing him to go with them (43:1-7).

We are grateful that Jeremiah had the courage to record some of his inner struggles and darker moments. This assures us that if God can use a person as human as Jeremiah, surely he can use us also, even with all our weaknesses.

Ezekiel

At first glance it may seem inappropriate to conclude a study of the humanity of the prophets with a look at the prophet Ezekiel. He was probably the strangest, the least human of all the prophets.[6]

It is difficult for us to identify with a man who experienced frequent visions. We do not feel completely comfortable with a man who was so perfectly self-controlled and committed to doing God's will that there was nothing he would not do that God asked of him. He refused to speak a single word for about seven and one-half years except to proclaim messages from God (Ezek. 3:26-27; 33:22). He allowed himself to be tied and bound for a total of 430 days (4:4-8). He submitted himself to ridicule and disgrace by shaving off his hair at God's orders (5:1-2). He controlled his grief, not shedding a tear when his wife died (24:15-18).

How then can we demonstrate the humanity of the prophets through the life of Ezekiel? The clue to discovering the human Ezekiel may reside in the title by which God addressed him.

God never did call Ezekiel by his name. He always addressed him as "son of man," ninety-three times to be exact. A great deal has been written to explain the significance of this title that is closely associated with Ezekiel. What does it mean, and why did God always use it when he addressed Ezekiel?

Commentaries have been in unanimous agreement that "son of man" refers to the mortality, weakness, and frailty of the prophet. He was only a member of the human race, a man and not God.[1] If this interpretation is correct, the purpose of the title was to remind Ezekiel of his lowliness and insignificance in contrast to the majesty of God. However, it seems strange that God would constantly belittle one whom he had created in his own image and, moreover, one called to be a prophet.

Also, it is significant that immediately after first addressing Ezekiel as "son of man," God ordered him to stand on his feet (Ezek. 2:1). The prophet had fallen flat on his face and was groveling in fear of the awesome vision of God at the river Chebar.

There seems to be a contradiction in reminding Ezekiel of his mortality and weakness (if that is what "son of man" means) and immediately afterward ordering him to stand on his feet. It is true that before one can stand before God he must fall down before him in submission. However, God does not want his followers to remain in that subservient position.

Therefore, because of this contradiction, we should look in another direction to find the true meaning of "son of man." Syntactically, in the Hebrew language "son of" expresses a construct relationship with the word that follows. Together they are the equivalent of the genitive or possessive case in English. As an example, "son of the king" means "the king's son." The construct word always expresses a relationship with the word that follows and is dependent on that word to complete its meaning.

"Son of" appears frequently in the Old Testament. It always denotes a relationship, such as a member of a group or class of people. Examples include "son of Abraham," "son of David," and "son of a prophet." The frequently used phrase "children of Israel" (Hebrew, literally, "sons of Israel") means that they were related to their ancestor Jacob (renamed Israel, Gen. 32:28). In every case in the Old Testament "son of . . ." denotes a relationship.

The word "man" that follows "son of" shows to whom he is related. "Man" is the Hebrew word 'adam. This word can be translated as "man" or as the proper name "Adam" in Genesis. It can also be understood in the collective sense of "mankind." Therefore, we conclude that "son of man" was God's way of saying, "Ezekiel, you are related to the human race (mankind)."

The phrase "son of man" also implies a relationship that requires responsibility. Because Ezekiel was a member of the human race, the title reminded him that he had a responsibility to other people. The Old Testament constantly emphasizes one's responsibilities to others. Cain tried to escape that responsibility with his question, "Am I my brother's keeper?" (Gen. 4:9).

The Israelite law provided for a kinsman-redeemer relationship (called go'el in Hebrew). This relationship placed certain responsibilities on a near kinsman. These included buying back family land that had been sold (Lev. 25:25), marrying the widow of a deceased brother if there were no children (Deut. 25:5-10), buying a kinsman out of slavery (Lev. 25:47-48), and avenging the death of a murdered relative (Deut. 19:6). Family responsibilities were clearly delineated by the Mosaic law from the earliest times in Israelite history.

The question of responsibility is echoed in the New Testament: "Who is my neighbor?" (Luke 10:29). The New Testament answer is that the "neighbor" is the person who acknowledges his relationship to the human family and accepts his responsibilities toward others.

There is further evidence of the implication of responsibility in the title "son of man." Shortly after first addressing Ezekiel by this title, God told him that he was to be a watchman to Israel (Ezek. 3:17; see also 33:7). The watchman was required to stand on the city walls to scan the horizon for approaching enemies. If he saw an invading army stirring up dust on the distant horizon, it was his duty to warn the people inside the city. They, in turn, would close the city gates and make preparations for defense. If the watchman went to sleep or was negligent in his responsibility of warning the people, the city would be taken by surprise and destroyed.

God told Ezekiel that he was to warn the people, and if he did not, their blood would be on his hands (3:20). Whatever else this solemn warning means, it reminds us in unmistakable language of our responsibility to warn others who may have strayed from God.

If we grant that the real meaning of "son of man" is not to be found in the idea of weakness and frailty, but in relationship and responsibility, why would God call Ezekiel "son of man"? The answer to this question, if correct, will justify our inclusion of Ezekiel in our discussion of the humanity of the prophets. The answer may be that Ezekiel, more than any other prophet, needed this constant reminder because he was truly the least human of all the prophets! He was austere, remote, a man of visions and trances, and not likely to be sought out at social gatherings. In fact, the very first time we meet him, he is all alone—sitting by the river Chebar and meditating—which may be what he enjoyed doing most!

Perhaps Ezekiel needed the constant reminder: "Ezekiel, you are part of the human race; you can't separate yourself from other people. You have a responsibility to your countrymen, and that is to deliver my messages of warning."

So whenever Ezekiel was inclined to shut himself away from other people in his "ivory tower," he would hear God say, "Son of man, get with it!" The words must have felt like pinpricks in the flesh of a man who by nature was retiring. Such a person would not relish the role that put him on center stage with words of warning and judgment for his people.

If the preceding interpretation of the Old Testament usage of "son of man" is valid, it opens up the possibility for fresh new insight into the New Testament usage of the same expression. Of all the terms used for Jesus,[8] his own favorite term for himself was "Son of man." It is found a total of ninety-four times in the New Testament. Where did he get the term? Evidently from his study of the Old Testament.

We look to the Old Testament for our answer. The term is found in Psalm 8:4 and Job 25:6, where it is parallel with "man," so it simply means "man" there also. It is also found in Psalm 80:17, but in the larger context (80:14-19) it is a figure for the nation Israel. Therefore, the New Testament usage could not have been derived from the Psalms or from Job.

Most scholars believe that Jesus took it from the one messianic occurrence in Daniel 7:13. It seems unusual, however, that a term used only once would be the one he would choose as his favorite.

Other scholars think he chose it because of its messianic usage in the book of Enoch. This was a noncanonical work written one or two hundred years before the time of Jesus. Again, it seems unlikely that he would pick a title from a book that was rejected from the sacred Scriptures by the Jewish community and that was probably never read publicly in the synagogues.

There is only one other place where Jesus would have observed the term "son of man," and that was in the book of Ezekiel.[9] Because of the frequent use of the word in Ezekiel, the most obvious New Testament link with the Old Testament should be sought in Ezekiel. If the term only means frail, weak, or mortal, then Jesus' usage seems to be strange and hard to explain. But what if he chose for himself the term applied to Ezekiel that suggested relationship and responsibility? If so, he gave it a new dimension of meaning by applying it to himself.

Jesus' willingness to humble himself and take on the form of a man (Phil. 2:7) and to identify himself with the human race and all that the incarnation represents was echoed every time he called himself "Son of man." It was as though he delighted in being identified with the human race!

The responsibility aspect is apparent in his willingness to accept the responsibility of redeeming mankind from its sins.

"The Son of man came to seek and to save the lost" (Luke 19:10, RSV).

Since the phrase "son of man" implies relationship and responsibility instead of mortality and weakness, no wonder Jesus' favorite designation for himself was "son of man."

Conclusion

What has been accomplished by emphasizing the humanity of the prophets? We have not intended to detract from them or to belittle them in any way by singling out their foibles and failures in this chapter. Rather, such a study accomplishes two positive results. First, it further assures us of the veracity and reliability of the Scriptures. If the biblical writers had intended to create legendary heroes for us, they would not have told us about their weaknesses and shortcomings. There is no attempt to "whitewash" the great men and women of the Bible. They are described with "warts and all." Abraham was willing to pass his wife off as his sister to save his own skin (Gen. 12:10-13); but God made a covenant with him, and he became the father of a great nation. Jacob was a despicable character, a trickster, and a liar; but he became Israel, the ancestor of all the tribes that composed the nation of Israel (Gen. 32:28). David had an affair with Bathsheba, but was called a man after God's own heart (Acts 13:22).

Rather than being embarrassed by these stories, we understand that they serve to remind us that the great figures of the Bible were subject to the same temptations as we are. Moreover, they remind us that the Bible tells the truth about them.

There is a second accomplishment of a study of the humanity of the prophets. It assures us that if God could work through imperfect, sinful, and weak people like some of the prophets we have read about, then he can surely use us for his purposes, also.

We do not have to become great and powerful persons, impervious to temptation, immune to fear and doubts, before God can use us. He called an eighty-year-old man, Moses, who probably thought his closing years would be spent in taking care of his father-in-law's flocks. He called a child named Samuel, a doubt-filled person like Jeremiah, and even a cold, austere Ezekiel. He could have chosen to give his revelation through angels stationed on every street corner to proclaim his word. He could have spoken through celestial loudspeakers placed at strategic points throughout the heavens. Instead, he chose to do his work through you and me.

Notes

1. Though not usually associated with prophets such as Isaiah, Jeremiah, and Amos, Moses was called a prophet (Deut. 18:15).

2. The Hebrew word used could mean that the bears killed the boys or simply slashed them with their sharp claws.

3. Preachers frequently use the story of Jonah's attempt to flee from the Lord as a parallel to their own struggle to resist their call to the ministry. However, the motivation is usually quite different. Jonah hated the rapacious Ninevites and did not want to share his God with them. Few people resisting a call of God to a preaching ministry have justified their refusal on the basis of hatred for lost people or an unwillingness to share their God with the lost!

4. It is unfortunate that Jeremiah is largely remembered for his weeping, a reputation probably earned on the basis of passages such as Jeremiah 9:1. He should be remembered for his courage, and apparently he was in later Jewish tradition. When Jesus asked his disciples, "Who do men say that the Son of man is?" one answer was "Jeremiah" (Matt. 16:14). The people saw courage and zeal in Jesus that they associated with Jeremiah.

5. Jeremiah 11:18-23; 12:1-6; 15:10-21; 17:12-18; 18:18-23; 20:7-18. These passages are called the "confessions of Jeremiah."

6. Ezekiel was so strange that at the height of the fad to explain all human behavior by Freudian analysis, it is not surprising that this prophet was subjected to the analyst's couch with some rather bizarre results. One scholar concluded that "Ezekiel exhibits behavioristic abnormalities consistent with paranoid schizophrenia . . . a true psychotic . . . periods of catatonia, the 'influencing machine,' a narcissistic-masochistic conflict, with attendant fantasies of castration and unconscious sexual regression, schizophrenic withdrawal, delusions of persecution and grandeur" [Edwin C. Broome, Jr., "Ezekiel's Abnormal Personality," *Journal of Biblical Literature*, vol. LXV, part 3 (September 1946): 291-92]. However, Broome concluded that it is not impossible to accept Ezekiel as a great religious, social, and political leader—even though he was mentally ill—and that his religious significance is by no means impaired by his paranoic condition!

It should have been apparent to men like Broome that, if a psychiatrist makes his analysis of a patient only after extensive periods of questioning in order to have a complete picture of the individual, a theologian should not make an analysis based on the few episodes preserved from the life of Ezekiel and from a distance of almost 2,600 years. A more realistic way to explain the unusual behavior of Ezekiel is to admit that anyone who unreservedly devotes himself to doing the will of God will likely be considered strange by most people.

7. An examination of thirty-four commentaries found them all to be in accord with this interpretation of "son of man."

8. There are many of such terms: Immanuel, prophet, priest, king, servant, Lamb of God, Son of God, the Christ.

9. Scholars have not given much consideration to Ezekiel as the source of the New Testament use of "son of man" because there is such unanimity about Daniel as its source. Alan Richardson, *An Introduction to the Theology of the New Testament* (New York: Harper & Brothers, 1958), pp. 145-146, has acknowledged the possible influence of Ezekiel on the "son of man" concept in the New Testament.

7

"The Just Shall Live by His Faith"
(The Faithfulness of the Prophet)

The prophets of Israel were a bulwark against the tide of immorality, faithlessness, and idolatry that engulfed the covenant people. By their steadfast faithfulness and their continual warnings to the people, they alone can be credited for saving Israel from total annihilation. But their task was not easy.

Lapses of Faith

One of the clearest reminders of the humanity of the prophets was their struggle to maintain the zeal of their own initial commitment. Men like Isaiah, Ezekiel, and Daniel apparently had little difficulty maintaining their early commitment. Other prophets, however, were not always so successful. As a result of the golden calf incident at Mount Sinai, God said he would no longer accompany Israel on her journey to the Promised Land. Moses thereupon boldly announced his intention of abandoning his own commitment: "If thy presence will not go with me, do not carry us up from here" (Ex. 33:15). Later he forfeited the privilege of entering the land with his people because of a single act of disobedience (Num. 20:1-12).

An unnamed prophet courageously denounced the altar of King Jeroboam, whereupon the king ordered him arrested. After witnessing his own hand shriveled by the prophet's power, the king relented and pleaded with the man of God to pray for him. As a gesture of desire for reconciliation, the king then invited the prophet to share a meal with him; but the prophet staunchly refused to have anything to do with the wicked king. However, shortly afterward this same prophet inexplicably was deceived by a lying prophet. He ate with him, in disobedience to a command of the Lord. In consequence of his lapse, he was killed by a lion (1 Kings 13:1-25).

Though he was not a prophet, Samson had been filled with the Spirit of God (Judg. 14:6). Later, however, the power of the Spirit departed from him because he revealed the secret of his strength to Delilah. He did not know "that the Lord had left him" (Judg. 16:20).

Little could be said to discredit the faithfulness of Samuel. Yet at least one time he found it difficult to obey God. That was in the matter of anointing a successor to Saul as king of Israel. Though Samuel was forced to announce to Saul that he had been set aside as king, he continued to grieve over Saul (1 Sam. 15:35). Finally, it was necessary for the Lord to upbraid him: "How long will you grieve over Saul, since I have rejected him from being king over Israel?" (1 Sam. 16:1, NASB).

The prophet who had the greatest difficulty remaining faithful to his task was Jeremiah. At least this was true in the earlier years of his ministry. Once he became so alienated from God that he determined never to speak another word in the Lord's name (Jer. 20:9).

These examples of the lapses of the prophets are rare and are not characteristic of them. Rather, the prophets are best remembered for their unwavering faithfulness to God even in the face of rejection, persecution, or death at the hands of their own people (Jer. 2:30).

Hebrew Meaning of Faithfulness

"Faith" or "faithfulness" comes from a Hebrew word *āman.* Its original meaning is uncertain. It once was believed to be from a word that means "to confirm" or "to support." More recently it has been linked to "secure" or "enduring," but even that is uncertain.[1] In the hiphil form (a causative verb in the Hebrew language) it affirms that one has confidence in someone else. It suggests that he trusts in that person or in that person's message. It is the same word from which our "Amen" comes. As an expression of approval or confirmation, "Amen" is found twenty-four times in the Old Testament.

Faithfulness has been defined as "a way of acting that grows out of inner stability."[2] It emphasizes "one's own inner attitude and the conduct it produces."[3] It is a type of behavior that may be described as "genuineness, reliability, conscientiousness."[4]

When an ancient Israelite heard the various words derived from the root āman, the idea that came immediately to his mind was "constancy." It is a word that accurately describes the Hebrew prophet in his relationship to God.

The Faithlessness of Israel

Many books have been written that speak about the "faith of Israel." However, they are usually describing the faith and commitment of the prophets rather than the faith of the people as a whole. Throughout its history Israel exhibited little true faith.

As has been noted previously, the history of Israel has rightly been called a "history of failure"—failure to be what God wanted her to be. The Israelites ignored the appeals of the prophets to return to God. The prophets repeatedly berated them for their faithlessness. The call to faithfulness was a mark of the true prophet as opposed to the false prophet (Deut. 13:1-3).

The prophets compared the faithlessness of the people to harlotry (Amos 7:17; Hos. 4:15; Isa. 1:21; Mic. 1:7; Jer. 2:20; 3:1; Ezek. 16:15-58; 23:5,19); fornication (2 Chron. 21:11; Isa. 23:17; Ezek. 16:15-16); adultery (Hos. 2:2; 7:4; Jer. 3:8-9; 13:27; 23:10; Ezek. 23:43,45), and prostitution (Jer. 13:27). Jeremiah and Hosea described Israel's faithlessness as "backsliding"[5] (Jer. 2:19; 3:6-8,11-12,14,22; 5:6; Hos.4:16; 11:17).

Throughout her history Israel's faithlessness to God was primarily due to the people's attraction to the idols of their pagan neighbors. These idolatrous rituals were usually accompanied by immoral sexual practices performed in the name of religion. The Israelites were unable to resist their carnal appeal.

God warned them even before they entered the land that they must drive out the native inhabitants. He knew that if the Canaanites remained in the land, Israel would be attracted to their gods and forget their covenant with him (Deut. 7:1-5; see also 4:15-31; 8:19; Ex. 20:4-6; Josh. 24:14-15,20). They had not yet come to the Promised Land when they were introduced to Baal of Peor, one of the gods of the Moabites. They quickly succumbed to the worship of Baal, thereby incurring the wrath of the Lord (Num. 25:1-5; 31:16).

From that time until after the return from exile in Babylon, Israel was never free from idol worship, with a few exceptions. There were rare times of religious reform, when the idols were destroyed by the king. Purges of the idols took place during the reigns of Hezekiah (2 Kings 18:1-6) and Josiah (2 Kings 22:1 to 23:25). However, their reforms never did reach the hearts of the people, for as soon as these kings died, the people reverted to their former idolatrous practices.

With the exception of a few of the kings, such as Hezekiah and Josiah, the prophets were almost alone in their struggle against the idolatry that characterized faithless Israel until the exile. Even after the years of punishment in exile (587-538 BC), the people did not return wholeheartedly to God. However, they did put away their idols during the exile. From that day to this, idol worship has not been a problem among the Jewish people, as it had been before the exile. The book of Malachi, a postexilic prophet, contains a graphic account of the continued faithlessness of Israel into postexilic times; but idolatry is not mentioned.

It would be impossible to enumerate all the passages in the prophetic books that speak about idolatry, for it was a major concern of the prophets. The fact that there are at least twenty Hebrew words that mean "idol" or "image" gives some indication of the frequent mention of idolatry in the Old Testament. The horror and repugnance toward idolatry on the part of the prophets is revealed in the Hebrew words. Almost without exception the words translated as "idol" or "image" come from words that mean weak or feeble (Isa. 2:8), a dung pellet (Ezek. 6:4), vapor or air (Jer. 8:19), horrible (1 Kings 15:13), twist or bind (Isa. 10:11), carve out (Isa. 40:19), detestable (2 Chron. 15:8; Jer. 7:30), decay or perish (1 Sam. 15:23; Zech. 10:2).

No other prophets ridicule idol worship quite so devastatingly as Isaiah (Isa. 40:18-20; 41:5-7,21-24,29; 44:9-20; 46:1-7) and Jeremiah (Jer. 10:1-16). They describe the foolishness of men who would go to the forest, cut down a tree, and use part of it for firewood and part of it to carve out an idol. The carved pieces of wood were covered with silver and gold. They were then clothed in expensive garments and fastened on pedestals with nails so they would not topple over. They were sometimes carried about in carts because they were unable to move about on their own power. Though people knew that the idol was the creation of their own hands, they would fall down and worship it and cry out, "Deliver me, for thou art my god!" (Isa. 44:17c).

An idol could do nothing—it could not help or harm a person because it was nothing (Jer. 10:5). It could teach nothing because it knew nothing. A person could not have fellowship with such a god because wood and stone cannot speak (Jer. 10:5). Jeremiah concluded, "They are worthless, a work of mockery;/In the time of their punishment they will perish" (10:15, NASB).

If idolatry is foolish, as Isaiah and Jeremiah so convincingly tell us, why do people worship idols? The question is deliberately phrased in the present tense because idol worship is still practiced. It is practiced in primitive societies just as it was in ancient times. But it is also found in "cultured" societies, though in more sophisticated forms. If a god may be defined as anything that is more important to a person than the Lord God, then there are many idolators among us.

Some of today's idols bear the names sex, pleasure, money, possessions, power, fame, knowledge, science, and reason. In fact, all these "gods" are manifestations of man's chief god, "self." The enthronement of self and the denial of God's lordship is the common sin of the human race that dates back to the Garden of Eden.

If idolatry is so patently ridiculous, why do people worship idols in this enlightened age? Answers to this question must include the following: First, man and woman are creatures who must worship something. The desire to worship is found in every level of civilization, however primitive or however advanced. Augustine recognized this distinctive characteristic of mankind when he said, "Thou hast made us for thyself, and our heart is restless till it finds rest in thee." The worship of a stone or a piece of wood is indicative of this basic characteristic of the human race, though it is perverted devotion and misses the mark of true worship.

A second appeal of idolatry is that a person wants to see what he worships. The highest level of religious experience is to understand that "God is spirit, and his worshipers must worship in spirit and in truth" (John 4:24, NIV). However, even among the disciples, who were close to our Lord, Thomas found it impossible to believe unless he could see (John 20:24). All of us think that it would be easier to believe if we could see. We forget that many did see Jesus and witnessed his miracles, yet refused to believe. Therefore, we cannot conclude that all intellectual doubts would be removed simply by seeing God.

A third explanation of idols is that a person would like to control his God or gods, whether he will admit it or not. It is easier to control what we can see than what we cannot see. In the ancient world it was commonly believed that the gods could be manipulated to work in behalf of the worshiper. Such control was believed attainable if the right sacrifices were brought, the proper ritual were performed, or the correct incantation were repeated. The idol always faced the veiled threat that it could be smashed into a thousand pieces or thrown in the fire if it did not produce results for its devotees.

A fourth explanation for the prevalence of idol worship throughout human history is the tendency of the natural person to want to degrade himself. Although created in the image and likeness of God, he has frequently chosen to worship stones or wood carved in the shape of animals that were created to serve him (Gen. 1:26). The apostle Paul recognized this inclination when he wrote:

"For although they knew God, they neither glorified him as God nor gave thanks to him, but their thinking became futile and their foolish hearts were darkened. Although they claimed to be wise, they became fools and exchanged the glory of the immortal God for images made to look like mortal man and birds and animals and reptiles. Therefore God gave them over in the sinful desires of their hearts to sexual impurity for the degrading of their bodies with one another. They exchanged the truth of God for a lie, and worshiped and served created things rather than the Creator—who is forever praised. Amen." (Rom. 1:21-25, NIV).

A fifth and final reason why people worship idols is implied in Paul's words cited above: Idols do not require holy conduct on the part of a worshiper. By contrast, the Lord demanded of his people, "You shall be holy; for I the Lord your God am holy" (Lev. 19:2b). By this demand, he introduced a revolutionary concept of moral and ethical content into the ancient understanding of holiness. Up to that time the word only meant "separation." A temple prostitute was considered "holy" in Canaan because the word only meant that the person was dedicated to the service of the deity.

In addition to the foolishness of worshiping a stick or stone, there are practical reasons why the making of images was absolutely prohibited in Israel (Ex. 20:4-6). One reason for the injunction against making idols is that it is impossible to capture the glory of God in all his fullness in any carved form. The totality of the nature, personality, and attributes of God cannot be depicted by the most talented artist, even by a Michaelangelo.

Therefore, any attempt to represent God in an art form (whether by painting or by sculpture) will always be less than successful.

Another reason for the prohibition of idols is that any carved or visual representation of God will tend to restrict our ability to think about God. This means that when we think of God, we will think of him in terms of art forms that have impressed themselves in our memory.

It can be demonstrated that all of us have unconsciously limited our cognitive concept of God through the influence of art forms by giving ourselves the following brief word association test. What is the mental image that comes to mind when you hear the word "Satan"? Is it a picture of horns, pitchfork, forked tail, and fiery nostrils? Why do you think this way about Satan? He is described in the Scriptures as one who masquerades in an attractive form—"an angel of light" (2 Cor. 11:14)—lest we be frightened and run from him. Isn't your image based on artists' concepts of Satan?

Try the test again with the word "angel." Does the word conjure up a vision of white robes, wings, halo, harp, and a puff of cloud surrounding the feet of an ethereal figure? Did you derive this image from the Bible or from artists' representations?

Try the test once more with "Jesus Christ." Which artist's head of Christ becomes your immediate mental image? Was it Holman, Rubens, Vandyke, Titian, or the work of another artist that has engraved itself in your mind? Try as we may, we cannot dissociate ourselves from these works of art. They have impressed themselves in our minds so indelibly that when we think of God, we are at once limited by them.[6] Imagine how difficult it would be to conceive of God in any terms other than his wood or stone image if we had that in front of us every time we worshiped him.

Another valid objection to making images of God is that what may have been intended as an aid to worship can become an object of worship. The average worshiper is not able to make such a fine distinction between the two concepts. It is erroneous to say that the worship of statues found in many Roman Catholic churches is sanctioned by official Catholic doctrine. These statues are intended to serve as aids to worship in the same way that stained-glass windows are.

However, if one has ever witnessed Catholic worship practices, particularly in the Latin American countries, he knows that the uneducated worshiper lavishes devotion on the statue or other relic of the church. He kisses it and genuflects before it, to the extent that it is an object of veneration for him. He is unable to make a distinction between form and reality.

A fourth reason for the biblical prohibition against making idols is that the worshiper, consciously or unconsciously, assumes an attitude of control over an image set on a pedestal in a church or on a shelf in the corner of his house. Our God, however, is a sovereign God who cannot be contained in any place by anyone. At the dedication of the Temple, Solomon acknowledged, "Behold, heaven and the highest heaven cannot contain thee; how much less this house which I have built!" (1 Kings 8:27).

A final reason for the prohibition of idols is suggested by the prophet Hosea: We become like that which we worship (Hos. 9:10). If we worship a dead stick or a lifeless stone, our religion will have no vitality. That which is without life cannot impart life to others. If we worship sex, we will become carnal. If we worship possessions, we will become materialistic. If we worship fame or power, we will become cruel and tyrannical. If we worship self, we will become vain and uncaring. Hosea accused his people of becoming as detestable as the idols they worshiped.

The prophets of Israel thoroughly understood the foolishness of idolatry and why it was so dangerous to the preservation of one's faithfulness to God. They knew that the covenant which God had made with Israel required that the people be faithful.

The Israelites were unable, however, to resist the allure of the pagan religious practices of their neighbors. They gave themselves freely to cultic practices that were abhorrent to God. The prophets realized that the people's continued faithlessness could lead only to ruin. They warned, pleaded, threatened, and berated them, but it was to no avail. Faithful prophets could not counteract the faithlessness of the people and their leaders (Ezek. 14:14).

Evidences of Loss of Commitment

A lesson that we should learn from Israel is that alienation from God does not happen in a moment. The abominable practices within the Temple itself described by Ezekiel did not happen overnight (Ezek. 8:1-18). The process is usually so gradual that a person is not aware that his own dedication has weakened. Then a time of testing reveals his unwillingness to act in conformity with the will of God.

Some years ago the evangelist Charles Finney composed a list of thirty-two evidences of what he called "backsliding in heart."[7] Some of his nineteenth-century language seems quaint today, but his premise was valid: It is easy to drift away from our commitment and hardly be aware of what has taken place. Therefore, we should take inventory from time to time to determine if our dedication has weakened and needs to be revitalized.

A checklist such as Finney proposed can be helpful. A briefer list than his should include at least the following as evidences of loss of commitment to the Lord:

1. Loss of interest in the Bible and in prayer
2. Serious doubt that the Bible is the Word of God
3. Unwillingness to do the will of God
4. Self-centeredness that reveals itself in such things as pride, hurt feelings, anger at being slighted by others, and envy
5. Fear of being thought different from other people if Christian principles are applied too conscientiously in daily life
6. Attraction to a worldly, secular way of life
7. Enjoyment of the company and activities of non-Christians more than Christians
8. Inordinate pride in personal achievement
9. No feeling of remorse over sins committed

10. A critical, unforgiving spirit toward people who have offended us.

At least once a year we ought to examine ourselves against these standards. If we find that the items on this checklist describe our attitudes and practices too accurately, it is time for repentance and renewed commitment (1 John 1:9).

Conclusion

The struggle of the prophets to remain loyal to the Lord in all circumstances is proof of their humanity. Our own struggle to maintain our commitment to the Lord is a reminder of our kinship to the prophets. Faithfulness is the best testimony of a believer before an unbelieving and skeptical world. "Be faithful, even to the point of death, and I will give you the crown of life" (Rev. 2:10, NIV).

Notes

1. Alfred Jepsen, "āman," in *Theological Dictionary of the Old Testament*, vol. 1, ed. G. J. Botterweck and Helmer Ringgren (Grand Rapids: William B. Eerdmans Publishing Company, 1974), p. 293.

2. Ibid., p. 317.

3. Ibid.

4. Ibid., p. 318.

5. "Backsliding" is from a Hebrew word that means "to turn." It is translated as "faithless" (NASB, RSV), "apostate" (NEB), "unfaithful" (TEV). The traditional KJV translation, "backsliding," is too colorful and descriptive to lose altogether. However, if maintained, the word "backsliding" should be understood as a deliberate act of alienation from God and not as a kind of careless, lazy sliding down into a tub filled with hot soapsuds!

6. This discussion should not be misinterpreted as a condemnation of art per se, which has enriched all our lives. It is intended to illustrate the consequences of trying to depict God in any visible form.

7. Charles G. Finney, *Lectures on Revivals of Religion* (New York: Fleming H. Revell Co., 1868), pp. 412-422.

8

"I Am with You"
(God's Presence with the Prophet)

In the preceding chapter the faithfulness of the prophet was examined. His struggles to remain loyal to the Lord were observed. A key to understanding his unwavering allegiance to God in spite of ridicule, physical abuse, and even death is found in a phrase that recurs time after time throughout the Old Testament: "I am with you." This was God's promise of his presence with the prophet.

It was the actual awareness of this presence that enabled the prophets to cope with the difficult situations which they constantly encountered. God's presence helped them to resist the temptation to leave their people and escape to a wayfarers' lodging place in the desert "to get away from it all' (author's paraphrase; see Jer. 9:2).

God's Presence as a Unifying Theme of the Bible

The question as to the central, unifying theme of the Bible has frequently been raised. By unifying theme we mean the common theme that holds the Bible together from the first verse of Genesis to the last verse of Revelation, despite the diversity of authorship and the hundreds of years that separate the first writings from the last. It has been estimated that at least a hundred different authors contributed to the writing of the Scriptures over a fourteen-hundred-year period.

There have been frequent critical onslaughts during the last century that would fragment the Scriptures and make them a poorly put together jigsaw puzzle. But in spite of these attacks, we sense that there is a remarkable underlying unity which is far more real than the cover that holds the pages together.

The central, unifying theme of the Bible has been identified in many ways. Some theologians say the sovereignty of God is the central theme—or, stated even more simply, God himself is the central theme. Some have posited the concept of the kingdom of God as the unifying theme. Others express it in terms of the lordship of God or the holiness of God. In recent years there has been an emphasis on the covenant as the unifying theme. In fact, it would be much more accurate to speak of the Old and New Covenants rather than the Old and New Testaments.

Some prefer to express the unity of the Bible Christologically—Christ hidden in the Old and revealed in the New Testament. Others feel that it is more appropriate to speak of the unity in terms of promise and fulfillment. By this they mean that the forward-looking promise of the Old Testament are realized in the New Testament. Others insist that the unity is found in redemption or salvation. Some have expressed the unity more dramatically as the scarlet cord or the trail of blood that runs through the Bible.

All of these are legitimate ways of understanding the unity of the Bible, but its unity can also be expressed meaningfully in terms of the presence of God.[1] Apart from salvation itself, this is perhaps the most comforting doctrine taught in the Scriptures.

The story of creation sets the stage for the presence of God. Genesis 1 suggests that this planet and the entire universe were created to serve as the backdrop for an encounter between God and man. The announcement of man created in the image and likeness of God should alert us to the theme of God's presence (Gen. 1:26-27). God would not make a creature like himself, only to set him adrift in an uncharted universe to be ignored and forgotten.

The first time the presence of God comes clearly into focus is in the Garden of Eden. There God came down in the cool of the evening to have face-to-face fellowship with the man and woman he had created.

Unfortunately, the Genesis story quickly becomes a scenario of creature running from God, a creature who has turned his back upon divine fellowship. There are a few rare exceptions along the way; for example, Enoch walked with God (Gen. 5:24). But the rest of the story is largely the account of man's flight from God and the divine pursuit.

God has withheld nothing to regain fellowship with alienated mankind—not even the withholding of his own Son. Throughout the rest of the Bible the promise of God's presence is given to those who will accept it. We are also frequently reminded of the rejection of his presence by those who did not value it. Among those who knew the presence of God were the prophets. Frequently, his presence was all that enabled them to keep going.

The Recurring Refrain

The phrase encountered throughout the Bible that more than any other proclaims the presence of God is the simple "I am with you." In the Hebrew language the phrase is reduced to two words: "I with-you." It was heard by the prophets and by many others during the course of Israel's history.

It is encountered first in Genesis 28 when Jacob fled from home to escape the wrath of his brother Esau, whom he had cheated out of the blessing that the aged Isaac had intended for the older twin (Gen. 27). Jacob lay down that first night away from home with a rock for a pillow. Cut off from home and familiar surroundings and faced with an uncertain future, he was probably not as self-assured as usual.

In a dream during the night he saw angels ascending and descending on a column to heaven. Since Jacob knew he merited only scorn from God, he must have been amazed to hear the reassuring words, "I am with you" (Gen. 28:15). It was as though God was saying, "I have a plan for your life, even though you are a scoundrel and don't deserve anything good from me."

Hundreds of years later the same assuring words were repeated when God appeared to Moses. Then eighty years of age,
he had resigned himself to living out his days as a lowly shepherd
with a nomadic Midianite priest and his family. God spoke to
Moses from a burning bush and told him that he had been
chosen to deliver Israel from Egyptian slavery. When Moses
objected that he was not qualified for the task, God gave him the
only assurance he needed: "I will be with you" (Ex. 3:12).

Later Moses keenly felt the need of God's presence. When it
appeared that the Lord would no longer accompany the Israelites on the journey to the Promised Land, Moses pleaded with
him, "If Thy presence does not go with us, do not lead us up
from here. For how then can it be known that I have found favor
in Thy sight, I and Thy people? Is it not by Thy going with us, so
that we, I and Thy people, may be distinguished frcm all the
other people who are upon the face of the earth?" (Ex.
33:15b-16, NASB).

When the twelve men sent by Moses to spy out the land of
Canaan returned, ten of them insisted that the inhabitants of the
land were too powerful to attack. They reported, "We seemed to
ourselves like grasshoppers" (Num. 13:33b, RSV). The Israelites
were demoralized and determined to choose another leader and
return to Egypt.

However, Joshua and Caleb, the remaining two spies sent
with the twelve, disagreed with the majority report. They
believed that the God who had promised the land to them would
give it to them. Joshua pleaded with the rebellious people, "The
Lord is with us; do not fear them" (Num. 14:9c), but the people
refused to believe him. Their refusal to believe that God's presence was all they needed to ensure victory cost them forty years
of wandering in the wilderness (Num. 14:29-34).

The tabernacle was another reminder of God's presence.
Throughout the years of desert wandering and for some years
after settling in the Promised Land, the tabernacle[2] served as a

visible symbol of the presence of God dwelling among his people.

At another critical time in the history of Israel, God again reminded his people of his presence with them. Moses had died, and a new, untested leader, Joshua, was about to lead the people into a land that was filled with unknown dangers. Just at this time Joshua heard the reassuring words, "Just as I have been with Moses, I will be with you" (Josh. 1:5b, NASB).

Years later the Israelites were suffering a time of oppression at the hands of the Midianites. God appeared at the winepress to a young man named Gideon to inform him that he had chosen him to shake off the yoke of the oppressor. As if to anticipate his objections, the angel of the Lord assured Gideon, "The Lord is with you, brave and mighty man" (Judg. 6:12, TEV; compare 6:16). It must be admitted that the words were not quite sufficient for Gideon. He required some signs before being absolutely convinced that God's presence was with him (Judg. 6:17,36-40).

The shepherd psalmist encountered all kinds of dangers while protecting his sheep from unseen threats lurking in every darkened crevice and behind every unturned stone. He came to depend upon the presence of God on the lonely hillsides. He voiced his confidence in words that have never been equaled for their inspiring quality of faith: "Though I walk through the valley of the shadow of death, I will fear no evil: for thou art with me" (Ps. 23:4, KJV).

God's Presence with His Prophets

The prophets were not the only ones who received assurance of the protecting presence of God. However, it was a reminder they needed and frequently received.

When God called Jeremiah to be his spokesman, the young man protested that he was too young and inexperienced for such a responsibility. God's answer was, "I am with you" (Jer. 1:8). Jeremiah would have many occasions to remember these words. When God told him not to marry (Jer. 16:2), when he was put in stocks by the priest Pashhur and subjected to public humiliation (Jer 20:2), and when he was put in a cistern to die (Jer. 38:6), he desperately needed the assurance of the presence of God.

Jeremiah knew God's presence, and he also spoke to Judah to assure the people that the Lord was with them, though they would not go unpunished (Jer. 30:11). The presence of God is all a person needs to proclaim God's message and to live God's way in the most difficult situations and in spite of one's own weaknesses.

It was a very critical period for Israel when the people had returned from their Babylonian exile and started rebuilding their nation. The assurance of God's presence came at such a time to the prophet Haggai to encourage the demoralized people. They did not have enough to eat or to wear and did not have adequate shelter against the extremes of the Judean weather (Hag. 1:4,6). Under the circumstances they were not really sure that God still loved them.

At such a critical time an unknown prophet, Haggai, appeared on the scene with the message of assurance he had received from God: "I am with you" (Hag. 1:13). Thus encouraged, the people redoubled their efforts and took up the work again of rebuilding the Temple.

However, hardly a month later their enthusiasm had evaporated. Some "sidewalk superintendents" who had remembered as children seeing the Temple of Solomon in all its glory were making unfavorable comparisons (Hag. 2:3). The new Temple was much smaller and less ornate, though it was the best the impoverished people could build. Consequently, some were saying that God would not be pleased by it and would refuse to honor it with his presence.

Again the reassuring words from the Lord were heard from the lips of the prophet Haggai: "I am with you" (Hag. 2:4). Strengthened by this promise, the people renewed their efforts and completed the Temple.

The prophet who linked the Old Testament to the New with the theme of the presence of God was Isaiah. It was another time of crisis for Judah. Israel and Syria to the north were threatening to invade Judah for not joining them in an alliance against Assyria.

The choices for Judah were not attractive. Judah could join with Israel and Syria and face almost certain destruction from the mighty Assyrian army. Or she could seek help from Assyria against the threat from Israel and Syria with no assurance that Assyria would protect Judah's rights.

In such a critical hour the prophet Isaiah went to King Ahaz of Judah and told him that God had a message for Judah. The prophet was willing to confirm his prophetic credentials by giving the incredulous king any sign he might ask for (Isa. 7:11).

The king would not ask for a sign. His refusal should not be interpreted as an act of pious faith but just the opposite—he had already sent word to Assyria asking for help. Consequently, he did not feel that he needed God's help. But Isaiah, being a true prophet, gave him a sign, anyway: "Therefore the Lord himself will give you a sign: The virgin will be with child and will give birth to a son, and will call him Immanuel" (Isa. 7:14, NIV).

Because attention has been focused on the virgin birth implications of this prophecy, little interest has been shown in the significance of the name Immanuel. However, Isaiah intended the name to be the heart of his message to King Ahaz. It means "God with us," and this was the sign Isaiah wanted to give the king. It meant that God was with Judah, so there was no need to fear foreign invasion from any direction. They could safely put their confidence in God. When God is with his people, it does not matter if all the armies of the world are gathered against them (see Rom. 8:31).

The Presence of God Reaffirmed in the New Testament

The New Testament takes up the Immanuel theme and lifts it to a new level with Matthew's announcement that Jesus' birth at Bethlehem was the fulfillment of Immanuel (Matt. 1:23). The presence of God which in times past had been partial and sporadic now had come to dwell with his people. In the incarnation the presence of God assumed the ultimate dimension of reality.

The human race has come to know the presence of God through the earthly life and ministry of Jesus in a way it had never previously experienced. In the person of Jesus God revealed his delight in fellowshipping with mankind. Jesus liked to be with people. He attended weddings and funerals. He eagerly looked forward to eating the last Passover meal with his disciples before his crucifixion (Luke 22:15).

The disciples experienced the presence of God through daily fellowship with his own Son, Jesus. On one occasion he promised them (and us): "Never will I leave you;/never will I forsake you" (Heb. 13:5, NIV). Just before his ascension Jesus assured his followers that the presence of God was not going to be removed because of his departure: "And surely I will be with you always, to the very end of the age" (Matt. 28:20b, NIV).

After Jesus' ascension the presence of God continued in the New Testament era through the indwelling presence of the Holy Spirit (John 14:16-17; 16:7).

Paul spoke of the continuing presence in terms of being "in Christ" (Eph. 1:3; Col. 1:28), "in him" (Eph. 1:11; Col. 2:6), and "Christ in you" (Col. 1:27).

The New Testament closes with the book of Revelation describing a future time when God will dwell in the midst of his people. No sun to give light and no temple in which to worship will be necessary, for his presence will be there (Rev. 21:22; 22:5). Even the name of new Jerusalem announced by Ezekiel speaks of the presence of God: "Yahweh Shammai." The title means "The Lord is there" (Ezek. 48:35).

Thus, from the first chapter of Genesis to the last chapter of Revelation, the theme of the presence of God courses like an everflowing stream.

Responses to the Presence of God

People respond differently to the promise of the presence of God. Some may experience a sense of false security that lulls them to believe that God will protect them and bless them whether they are faithful or not. This was the tragic error of ancient Israel that the prophets could not overcome, in spite of all their warnings. False prophets were assuring them that everything was all right because of the Temple in their midst. "The temple, . . . the temple," they told the people (Jer. 7:4). The Temple was a visible symbol of the presence of God. Therefore, the Israelites believed that in spite of idolatry, immorality, and faithlessness of every kind, God continued to be with them.

They missed the point of one of Ezekiel's warning visions when he described the glory of the Lord departing from the Temple and leaving the city (Ezek. 11:22-23). Later he assured them that God would return after a time of purging by the same way he had departed (43:2).

Israel's lessons should not be lost on us—we cannot presume on the continued presence of God. A Christian's sins cause him to feel separated from God. So we are warned, "Do not quench the Spirit" (1 Thess. 5:19).

Another response to the presence of God is that of fear accompanied by a desire to flee from him. Adam sinned and hid from God (Gen. 3:8,10). Amos described the person who was terrified by the thought that there was no place he could escape from God: "Though they dig into Sheol,/From there shall My hand take them;/And though they ascend to heaven,/From there will I bring them down./And though they hide on the summit of Carmel,/I will search them out and take them from there;/And though they conceal themselves from My sight on the floor of the sea,/From there I will command the serpent and it will bite them./And though they go into captivity before their enemies,/From there I will command the sword that it slay them,/And I will set My eyes against them for evil and not for good" (Amos 9:2-4, NASB).

In the ancient world the idea of fellowship with a loving God was almost incomprehensible. Gods were fearful beings to be appeased and kept at a distance. The Babylonian creation story says that man was created to do the work of the gods so they could spend their time in rest and play. There is no suggestion that the gods thought highly of the human race. Nor were they particularly interested in helping lowly human creatures.

It was believed that one must bring costly offerings in order to get the attention of the gods for the purpose of presenting one's petitions. What more costly gift could a devotee bring than his own child? This kind of logic resulted in the widespread practice of human sacrifice in the ancient Near East. However, a person could never draw near in loving, confident trust to a god like Molech of the Ammonites or Chemosh of the Moabites after his children had been taken by the god as sacrifices. There could only be fear and sullen resentment of such gods.

Little girls were buried alive by their fathers as sacrifices to the gods; their sons were slaughtered to appease the gods. The highly civilized Carthegenians would buy children from poor people and slaughter them for sacrifice as one would a bird or a lamb.

Try to imagine a typical sacrificial scene. The bronze statue of the god Kronos was placed at the edge of a pit filled with fire. His outstretched metallic arms extended over the fire with upright palms, tilted slightly downward. The red hot arms would receive the child and drop it into the fire below. Musicians surrounded the altar and played their instruments loudly to drown out the screams of the victims. Could anyone draw near in loving trust to a god who demanded such offerings? The presence of the gods in the ancient world only invoked fear and dread in the hearts of the people.

By contrast, instead of demanding the sacrifice of our sons and daughters, God gave his own Son as a sacrifice to atone for all our sins. Such a God was not known outside of Israel in the ancient world.

There is a third response to the thought of the presence of God: the response of gratitude. The psalmist considered the inescapable presence of God, and it brought praise and gratitude to his lips (Ps. 139:7-12). Compare Amos 9:2-4, where with similar words the rebellious sinner considered the inescapable presence of God and was afraid.

Sometimes a person does not consider how his or her rejection of God's presence grieves God. Perhaps it is impossible to understand just how deeply God is hurt by one's rejection of him. Only the person who has offered his love to another, and had his love hurled back in his face with callous indifference, can understand.

It is easy to overlook those verses that reveal with almost human candor the emotional response of God to our rejection of him. Ezekiel reported the feelings of God: "I have been broken by their adulterous hearts."[3]

Jesus wept over Jerusalem: "How often I have longed to gather your children together, as a hen gathers her chicks under her wings, but you were not willing!" (Luke 13:34, NIV).

Some have even suggested that the blood and water that gushed from the side of Jesus on the cross (John 19:34) show that he died of a broken heart. Whether this interpretation of organic rupture is correct, it is true that he died of a broken heart (as we use this idiom). He still weeps when you and I reject him today.

What His Presence Does for Us

The question that must be raised in any discussion of the presence of God is: "Why is God's personal presence needed?" What does his presence do for us? Wouldn't it be sufficient just to know that there is a God who created us, takes care of us, and will bring us into his presence someday? Why should we actually experience his presence now?

The most obvious answer to questions like these is that we need the presence of God. In every case already cited in this chapter where God appeared to someone and said, "I am with you," that occurred in answer to a particular need of that person. Or it may have been the response to a crisis that affected not only one person but sometimes the entire community. Jacob,

Moses, Joshua, Gideon, Isaiah, Jeremiah, and Haggai all heard "I am with you" in a time of desperate need.

Those who have experienced serious illness or a personal family crisis or tragedy; those who have been misunderstood or rejected; those who are lonely or have stood beside the open grave of a loved one understand the necessity of the presence of God. A Christian, having experienced the strength and help of God in such difficult hours, wonders how unbelieving people can ever cope with similar situations without the supportive presence of God.

Difficult times are not the only times God's presence is needed. When we are endeavoring to do something worthwhile, we discover that we need his presence if we are to succeed. The sense of need is felt especially when we may be doing something that promotes the kingdom of God. Jesus said, "Apart from me you can do nothing" (John 15:5).

A second contribution of the presence of God to our lives is that his presence makes us different from all other peoples upon the face of the earth (see Ex. 33:16). How many times has that indefinable quality of divine presence been expressed in words like these: "I saw something in that person I did not have and had not previously seen in others. It made me dissatisfied with myself, and I wanted the peace and happiness that person obviously had." It is the awareness of the presence of Christ in another person that has led countless thousands to begin a search to find that same presence for themselves.

A final contribution of the presence of God is that it assures us of his love. The comparison may be trite, but it is valid to say that we like to be with a person we love. We think about that one when we are separated and can hardly wait to be reunited.

In short, the presence of God is the best description of his love for the human race that can be found in the Bible. He loved us so much that he gave his only Son as a sacrifice to redeem us (John 3:16). Just as we want to be constantly with the person whom we love, so God wants to be constantly with us throughout eternity because he loves us so much. However, in our moments of perfect candor with ourselves, we know we are not so lovable that anyone should want to be around us forever! We find ourselves overawed and must ask as did the psalmist, "What is man, that you think of him?" (Ps. 8:4a, TEV).

The answer to that question is given from the beginning to the end of the Bible. It begins with God in the midst of a garden and ends with him in a new garden surrounded by his people. God has a continuing love affair with the human race that is apparent through the pages of the Old Testament. The prophets were aware of that presence and frequently announced it to others.

The doctrine continues to be affirmed in the New Testament from the incarnation of Jesus in Bethlehem to the future consummation of the ages. His presence is not something to be experienced in some far-off future time; it is a present reality. Yet in a special way every Christian waits for the time when he will see God face to face (1 John 3:2).

Perhaps the apostle Paul was reflecting on God's presence, which he had experienced throughout his ministry, when he said, "For to me, to live is Christ and to die is gain" (Phil. 1:21, NIV). He had known the constant presence of Christ in his travels about the Mediterranean world, whether he was before rulers, in prison, being beaten, or shipwrecked. He anticipated knowing the presence even more fully in the future because at best the presence of God experienced in this life is partial and incomplete. "Now we see only puzzling reflections in a mirror, but then we shall see face to face" (1 Cor. 13:12, NEB).

Notes

1. See Samuel Terrien, *The Elusive Presence: Toward a New Biblical Theology* (New York/San Francisco: Harper & Row, Publishers, 1978).

2. "Tabernacle" is from a Hebrew word that means "to dwell." The word itself speaks of the dwelling presence of God.

3. This is a literal translation of Ezekiel 6:9. See also Jeremiah 4:19-22; 8:18 to 9:2, which are interpreted by many as expressions of Jeremiah grieving and weeping over the sins of Israel. Notice, however, that in the larger context of each of these passages, reference is made to "my people." "My people" is the language God uses to refer to his covenant people. Therefore, it probably means that God is the speaker in these verses rather than Jeremiah. If so, it is God who is broken by the sins of his people (Jer. 8:21). Ezekiel 6:9 and Jeremiah 8:21 anticipate the cross in their pathos. See also Isaiah 53:3-4 and Hosea 11:8-9, which also reveal the grief of God for the sins of his people.

9

"Behold, Days Are Coming"
(The Idealism of the Prophet)

Like a physician who probes the arm in search of a vein in which to insert the hypodermic needle, Satan is always probing to find a Christian's weakest point. For each person it is different. One person may not be tempted at all by the desire to steal; but he turns pale green with envy when his next-door neighbor gets a new automobile, while he has to drive his old model for another year. Another may not be tempted to commit adultery but looks with lustful glance at his neighbor's wife or lives out his fantasies by reading pornographic literature.

However, the most devastating point at which Satan probes us and where very often he finds our Achilles' heel is at the point of motivation: "Why do you serve God? You don't expect anyone to believe that people serve God only because they love him or that they have no thought of reward for themselves?" (compare Job 1:9-11).

Satan does not believe that any of us is such an idealist that we reverence and serve God just for himself. He would say that such altruism is impossible, but most of the prophets in the Old Testament were living denials of such cynicism. Their confidence in God never wavered regardless of outward circumstances.

Even when they were rejected by their own people, they remained committed to the proclamation of the word of the Lord. Though life was often brutal and thankless to them, they remained unreconstructed idealists in a world that labeled them foolish, impractical visionaries, and dreamers. They continued to hold out hope for a people who seemed hopelessly marked for destruction.

Samuel

Samuel would be called an idealist by today's standards. He believed that Israel should continue under the theocratic rule of God. The people, however, preferred to have a king like their neighbors. Samuel tried to warn them that a king would conscript their sons for his army. He would take their daughters to be perfumers, cooks, and bakers. He would seize the best of the fields, the vineyards, and the olive groves of the people to give them to his servants and would make slaves of the people (1 Sam. 8:11-18).

But despite Samuel's warnings, the Israelites insisted on having a king. For them the direct rule of God seemed too idealistic and impractical in a world accustomed to the pomp and power of kings. People still are willing to give up their freedom for the promises of governments to protect and provide for them from the cradle to the grave.

Properly understood, a church is a theocracy, not a democracy. When a vote is taken in a business meeting, the congregation usually understands that they are seeking to find the will of the majority. But this belief is erroneous. The majority may be wrong. The minority who voted against the proposal may actually be right. Sometimes neither may be reflecting the will of God. A church vote ideally should never be divided, for the will of God is not divided. A divided vote indicates that all have not prayed sufficiently to find God's will. God's rule in Eden was theocratic. God's rule of the church is theocratic. The book of Revelation closes with a description of the restoration of God's rule over the earth with all its inhabitants acknowledging his lordship.

When Samuel saw that Israel was set on having a king rule over them, he gracefully stepped aside as God's theocratic leader over the people. God had told him, "They have not rejected you but they have rejected me" (1 Sam. 8:7). Could such a charge be leveled at any of our churches today?

Hosea

Hosea was crushed by the faithlessness of his wife. He could very easily have become cynical and asked, "What's the use of serving God?" But instead, he came to understand God's love and forgiveness for Israel through his personal sorrow. Hosea witnessed the violence of the priests (Hos. 6:9) and the wickedness of the people (Hos. 7:1) and the king (Hos. 7:3-7). He abhorred Ephraim's dependence,[1] like a silly dove, upon Egypt and Assyria (Hos. 7:11) rather than upon God. He warned the people that they had forgotten God (Hos. 8:14), but he still pleaded with them, "Return, O Israel, to the Lord your God" (Hos. 14:1).

Hosea was typical of the idealistic prophet who never became cynical, disillusioned, discouraged, or lost hope. The realist would have looked at Hosea's world and concluded that life in Israel was a parody of what God intended it to be—sensual, cruel, proud, grasping, and immoral. Indeed, Israel had forgotten her God and lost her way. Under such circumstances it would have been easy enough to conclude that Israel was not worth saving. But Hosea did not give up hope. He continued to plead, "Return, O Israel."

Amos

The prophet Amos, with his unrelenting messages of doom and judgment, might scarcely be considered an idealist or a man of hope. He was a realist about Israel. He did not allow them any false hopes. He warned those who expected the Day of the Lord to be a time of vindication of Israel and of judgment upon her enemies that they were mistaken. He said it was going to be a day of gloom for Israel, for God was going to judge Israel as well as her enemies (Amos 5:18-20).

However, Amos never did give up believing that his people could repent and return to God. Therefore, in the midst of his warnings of doom, we find him pleading with them to seek the

Lord (Amos 5:6,14). Amos was enough of an idealist to believe that it was never too late for an individual or a nation to return to God.

The book of Amos closes with an expression of hope unexcelled in the Old Testament for descriptive beauty (Amos 9:11-15). In fact, the verses are quite different in spirit and content from what has preceded. Many Old Testament scholars do not believe they could have been written by the same person who uttered the messages of doom found in the rest of the book.

Furthermore, some of these scholars go so far as to say that no prophet preached messages both of judgment and hope. Where they find both emphases in the same book, they insist that they were from different sources. However, rather than being the exception, this dual emphasis is typical of the prophets.[2] They did not delight in denouncing their people. They constantly searched for that spark of goodness in Israel that could be kindled.

The idealist looks for the best instead of the worst in others. The prophets did not think it incongruous to hold out hope for a restored Israel and in the same breath to denounce them for their sins.

Micah

Micah could also be added to the list of prophets whose idealism permitted him to say, "Who is a God like thee, pardoning iniquity/and passing over transgression/ . . .? He does not retain his anger for ever/because he delights in steadfast love./He will again have compassion upon us" (Mic. 7:18-19a).

This was the same prophet who also warned: "Its heads give judgment for a bribe,/its priests teach for hire,/its prophets divine for money;/ . . . Therefore because of you/Zion shall be plowed as a field; Jerusalem shall become a heap of ruins" (Mic. 3:11-12). Only an idealist could say about Israel in Micah's time: "The lame I will make the remnant;/and those who were cast off, a strong nation" (Mic. 4:7).

The idealist has the remarkable gift of seeing unrealized potential in another person and therefore encourages that person to achieve his potential. This kind of idealism ought to characterize every Christian, for wasn't it the confidence in us and love that Jesus expressed for us that drew us to him in the first place? He made us aware that he could make our lives meaningful and worthwhile if we would give ourselves to him. Because of our own experience, we ought to be sensitive to the potential in other people. We should encourage them to develop their latent abilities. The encourager is needed more than breakers of bruised reeds or quenchers of dimly burning wicks (see Isa. 42:3).

Instead, however, we sometimes look at the outward appearance and miss what lies beneath the surface (1 Sam. 16:7). Would we have had the spiritual discernment to choose as Israel a devious young man named Jacob, who stayed at home with his mother? Would we not have chosen Esau, the sturdy outdoorsman? Would we have been able to pick weeping Jeremiah out of a crowd as God's prophet in Jerusalem? Would we have looked at vacillating, impetuous Peter and called him a rock?[3]

Jesus did not look at people from the perspective of how they could serve him or how he could manipulate them to do something for him. Rather, he always tried to mend broken, shattered lives and to bring them to their fullest self-realization (see John 8:3-11; compare Isa. 42:3; 61:1).

This is idealism at its most sublime. It ought to characterize every Christian. We ought to look for the potential for good in other people and consider what they can become in Christ. When we do, we will no longer condemn them for what they are.

Habakkuk

Habakkuk, though one of the lesser known prophets, delivered one of the most idealistic affirmations of faith found in the Scriptures.

He prophesied at a time when it would have been much easier

to be a pessimist than an optimist about the future of Judah. The Babylonians were beating their war drums when Habakkuk appeared on the scene. They were marching against smaller nations, plundering them and sweeping by like the wind with no one hindering them. With the threat of the destruction of Judah a reality, Habakkuk affirmed his confidence in God: "Though the fig tree should not blossom,/And there be no fruit on the vines,/Though the yield of the olive should fail,/And the fields produce no food,/Though the flock should be cut off from the fold,/And there be no cattle in the stalls,/Yet I will exult in the LORD,/I will rejoice in the God of my salvation" (Hab. 3:17-18, NASB).

Perhaps a paraphrase of the prophet's words would capture the incredible daring of his faith more clearly for a twentieth-century reader: "Though I didn't get the raise I was expecting, the medical bills are ruining me, and the finance company repossessed my car and new color TV, yet I will still rejoice in the Lord!" True faith is an "in-spite-of" commitment. It is not dependent upon favorable circumstances.

Jeremiah

If an idealist is a person who can express hope for the future in spite of present circumstances, then any list of Old Testament idealists would have to include Jeremiah. At the outset he did not think that he was qualified to be a prophet (Jer. 1:6). He experienced periods of depression and even accused God of mistreating him. However, Jeremiah must have developed an indomitable spirit of idealism, for he continued preaching for forty years without a favorable response from his people.

Though we ordinarily identify Jeremiah with messages of warning and impending judgment upon Judah, some of the most inspiring messages of hope for the future came from the lips and actions of this prophet. He believed in the people of God, though they did not reciprocate his feelings.

Jeremiah's hope for the future was expressed in many concrete ways. He purchased a piece of property during the worst of the siege of Jerusalem as a dramatic expression of his confidence in the future (Jer. 32:1-15). Real-estate values at such a time would have been at an all-time low. Imagine what property would sell for in your hometown if an invading army had encircled it and the town's fall was imminent!

He chose to remain with his people in devastated Judah rather than accept Nebuchadnezzar's tempting offer to go to Babylon, where he could have lived in comfort on a royal pension. He might have reasoned, "This is God's reward to me for my years of faithfulness."

Even while speaking words of judgment, he mingled them with words of hope for the future for those who would listen. Once he spoke about Judah in terms of two baskets of figs, one good and one rotten. The rotten figs[4] were those who remained in Jerusalem. The good figs were those who were taken to Babylon, where they would be protected. Those in exile would form the remnant of a people that God would bring back to rebuild the land after seventy years (Jer. 24:1-10; 29:10-14).

The messianic passages of the Old Testament all imply that there is hope for the future. Some of Jeremiah's utterances would appropriately be classified as messianic. Though not as closely identified with messianic promises as the prophet Isaiah, nonetheless Jeremiah spoke of an ideal ruler in an age to come (Jer. 23:5-6; 33:15-16; 30:8-9,21). Jeremiah believed in the future of Israel, and he believed that it would be realized under a descendant of King David.

The most profound statement of hope in the future found in the book of Jeremiah was his pronouncement of a new covenant that God was going to make with his people (Jer. 31:31-34).

The covenant is unquestionably the most important theme in the Old Testament. Jeremiah's announcement of a "new covenant" (besides being the only use of this phrase in the Old Testament) is probably the single most important prophetic utterance by Jeremiah during his forty-year ministry.[5]

Jeremiah made it clear that God would take the initiative in establishing the new covenant with his people. Notice that the personal pronoun "I" is used of God ten times in the brief passage. Its frequent repetition serves as a constant reminder of God's initiative. The new covenant would be distinguished from the old covenant by its inwardness—that is, God's law would be written on the hearts of his people, not on tables of stone. People would obey God because they wanted to, not because they had to. The new covenant would be experienced on a personal basis—each person, from the greatest to the least, would know the Lord. It would be a covenant based on God's forgiveness of the people's iniquities.

This idealistic relationship between God and his people is nowhere else in the Old Testament described more eloquently. Christians insist that Jeremiah's prediction of a new covenant has been fulfilled in Christ.

Ezekiel

Ezekiel was another prophet who exhibited the traits of an idealist. Before the fall of Jerusalem, like Jeremiah, he preached messages of warning about God's impending judgment on his people. Like Jeremiah, he found that no one listened to him.

Word finally came to Babylon, where he lived, that Jerusalem had fallen, just as he had predicted (Ezek. 33:21). Having been vindicated as a true prophet, it would have been tempting for Ezekiel to spend the rest of his life exulting, "I told you so! You should have listened to me!" But instead, he immediately shifted to a constructive message about the possibilities for the future. A defeated, downtrodden people did not need to be reminded of the hopelessness of their situation. They needed a word of encouragement about the future. So in the closing chapters of the book of Ezekiel (Ezek. 40—48) we find the description of a vision of a new Temple, a people restored to its land, healed of its afflictions, purged of its sins, and faithful to the Lord. Even the name of Jerusalem would be changed to "The Lord is there" (Ezek. 48:35). The new name would serve as a constant reminder to the people of the protecting presence of God in their midst.

Are There Idealists Today?

In our own times, how does one remain an idealist in a world filled with violence, hatred, brutality, and the smell of doom in the air? How does he maintain hope for the future? Can a sensitive, compassionate person who is more concerned about human values than personal profit succeed in today's business and professional world? Can a Christian succeed in today's world without compromising his principles? Can young people find any heroes in today's world, when every idol has been tarnished and when it is difficult to believe there really is a genuinely "good" person? The media are obsessed with the presentation of life as ugly, brutal, sensual, and futile. Even some Christians have become so saturated by this kind of "neorealism" that somehow they think they are missing out if they are not experiencing what others tell them is "real life." It would be very easy to become cynical and pessimistic in today's world.

The Old Testament prophets could surely have sympathized with the person today who tries to keep things in proper perspective when there is so little reason for remaining optimistic about the future.

We live in a world of brutal realities; and whether we like it or not, power is the name of the game. Whether we call it political, ethnic, or atomic, the amount of power that can be mustered frequently determines the outcome of events. The moral rightness of an issue at stake does not guarantee its success. There seems to be no room for idealistic dreamers in the nuclear age, when man has the capacity—and sometimes, it seems, the desire—to blow himself off the face of the earth with one immense cosmic blast. And if he is not bent on outright destruction of his environment, he sometimes seems determined to pollute it until it is uninhabitable.

We automatically react against this ugly picture of the world and insist that Christians, like the prophets of old, are idealistic about the future. However, it may be necessary to check up on our idealism from time to time. We may discover that some of the mood of cynicism and hopelessness that has engulfed the world has also rubbed off on us. It is not easy to maintain the idealism of one's initial commitment to the Christian faith. At first it was easy to love everybody, to see the best in the worst of people, and to have high hopes for the future. But what about now?

Israel in the time of Haggai must have experienced this same kind of idealistic fervor about the future. With Haggai's encouragement, the people rebuilt the Temple that had been destroyed by Nebuchadnezzar. They believed that the messianic age would be ushered in when they completed the work. They were convinced that Israel would again become a respected, affluent power among the nations.

However, things did not work out as they had anticipated. Life continued to be grim in Judah, and survival was difficult. Also, the nation was still under Persian domination. With the passing of years, the people became disillusioned. Their idealism about the future vanished and was replaced by a cynical attitude about the justice of God (Mal. 2:17; 3:13-15). They questioned whether God loved them (Mal. 1:2-5). Their worship practices were replaced by carelessness and indifference to worship, even on the part of the priests (Mal. 1:6-13).

Perhaps a description of an idealist that would embrace both Old Testament prophet and contemporary man is in order. The idealist is not a blind Pollyanna, who tightly folds his robes about him to avoid contamination. He does not refuse to see the world as it is. The Christian idealist, like Habakkuk (3:17-18), has an "in-spite-of" faith. In spite of circumstances he does not become cynical or disillusioned, and he never gives up on the world or his fellowman.

He continues to love, though he may not be loved in return. He continues to serve others, though very few seem to appreciate his service. He still confirms the sovereignty of God, though it may appear that Satan has already won the day. He does not spend his time in self-pity, saying, "I'm lonely, unloved, depersonalized, dehumanized; and no one cares what happens to me." He does, however, seek to minister to those who do feel that way.

Each of us should be committed to being a Christian idealist. In this way we can best preserve the spirit of the prophets who were idealists about the future. We can anticipate a rebuff by a "realistic" world that will say, "Foolish, impractical, visionary." When we idealistically offer Christ as the solution for the world's problems, we can expect to hear: "Wishful thinker, unwilling to face reality."

Similar slurs were cast at the Old Testament prophets when they told the people to put their trust in God (Hos. 9:7; Jer. 29:26). Jeremiah told them that the only way the nation could be saved would be to follow God's order and to submit to the Babylonians. For his advice he was called traitor, liar, false prophet, and worse (Jer. 20:8;10; 26:11; 38:4).

Several years ago Baptists in Brazil conducted an evangelistic campaign throughout that great land with the theme, "Christ, the only hope." Skeptics scoff at what they consider to be an oversimplified solution for the world's problems. Even some Christians are embarrassed by such sweeping generalities. However, the more an unbelieving world struggles to solve its problems without Christ, the more deeply it sinks into the morass of despair and hopelessness. Will it ever learn that Christ really is the *only* hope?

A realist is a person who understands what life really is and how it ought to be lived. If this definition is correct, the Christian probably has a better understanding of the world than anyone else. He is the only authentic realist because he knows himself, and he knows the nature of man. He has no illusions about his own weaknesses or needs. He can say with the French essayist Montaigne, "I've never met a greater monster or miracle than myself."

The Christian realist knows that man is a sinner. He understands that sin is not just a psychological aberration of a morbid mind entrapped in its Victorian past. He knows that guilt cannot be eliminated by telling ourselves over and over that there is no such thing as sin. The world in which we live believes that man is basically good and that, given the opportunity, he can solve his problems and create an ideal society. The Bible gives us a different picture of man. It depicts *homo sapiens* as a sinner, so self-centered that he will never be able to create an ideal, caring society.

Since the Christian idealist is more accurate in his assessment of the nature of man, he is in a better position to offer workable solutions. Not only does he know that man is a sinner; he also believes that man is created in the image of God. Therefore, he affirms the value of every person regardless of his race, color, or background.

The unregenerate person places a very low price tag upon other people, despite his protestations to the contrary. If we want to know the value mankind places on each other, all we need to do is to read the headlines of brutality, corruption, and violence in the daily newspapers. If we want to know the value that God places on mankind, we need to read the account of Jesus Christ and his cross and grasp its significance.

The cross is the ultimate expression of idealism. It declares God's unyielding conviction that man is a worthwhile creature who can achieve meaningful life. Therefore, the Christian, having experienced God's love and grace for himself, knows that every person has the same potential for redemption and wholeness of life.

The Christian idealist is totally involved in his world because he is convinced of the potential for good in every person. Therefore, like the prophets of old, he must be in the marketplace proclaiming the Word of the Lord. Even though all will not hear him or be transformed, he knows that some will.

In his zeal for sharing his faith, it is imperative for a Christian to maintain a careful distinction between involvement in the world and identification with it. The prophets of the Old Testament and, of course, Jesus in the New Testament are our models for this differentiation. Some voices tell us that if we are to communicate the good news to people we must "identify" with them. We know what they mean—swim in their cesspool, do the same immoral things that they do, read the same pornographic literature, satisfy the same carnal desires.

However, you do not save a drowning person by "identifying" with him. You save him by becoming involved with him where he is. You do not thrash around in the water to assure him that you are not a better swimmer than he is. Nor do you go under a couple of times to give him confidence that you understand his problem and that you accept him as he is. No! Because you understand his situation so thoroughly, your only thought is to get him out of the water. The only way you can help him is through involvement, not identification.

Some have argued that Jesus "identified" himself with the world so successfully that his enemies had reason to accuse him of being a glutton and a drunkard. The person who defines Jesus' "identification" in these terms needs to read the passage again (Luke 7:34). What Jesus was saying was that "this generation is saying these things about me." But the accusations made against him were untrue.

For a more accurate assessment of Jesus, we should ask the apostle Peter. From close personal observation he had a better opportunity than most to form an unbiased assessment of Jesus. His conclusion was, "You are the Christ, the Son of the living God" (Matt. 16:16, NIV).

Sometimes there is a confused mixed-up appeal, made especially to young people, that says: "Isn't it great to be a Christian? You can become one and not even your best friend will detect the difference!" The appeal seems to suggest that one can become a Christian without the inconvenience of changing one's life-style.

The question that fairly shouts for an answer to this kind of appeal is: "If becoming a Christian makes no changes in one's life, then why bother to become one?" We must remember that there will always be tension between the Christian and the world in which he lives because he is trying to push the world in one direction, but the world doesn't want to go that way. He may even feel like a person who has turned on the freeway during the five o'clock rush going the wrong way because there seem to be so few going the same direction as he. The prophets experienced the same kind of tension and pressure as they tried to point Israel in a different direction from the one she was pursuing.

True, the Christian idealist will be called simplistic, foolish, nonintellectual, impractical, and visionary. There will be times when he will be almost tempted to give up his idealistic commitment to changing the world through Jesus Christ. Jeremiah and other prophets had similar moments of discouragement (Jer. 20:9).

An examination of some qualities of Jesus will help to restore idealism at those times when it seems to waver. Jesus was surely an idealist; he never became cynical or disillusioned and never gave up on the human race.

One quality that helped him to keep going was his acceptance of the role of the servant who never got tired of serving (instead of wanting to be the master served by others).

The initial all-out commitment and enthusiasm of a new Christian is sometimes dampened when he discovers that other people do not appreciate his good intentions. They reject his message, and the world seems to remain unchanged. At such a time it is well to recall that a Christian is a servant. The servant (or slave, as he would more accurately have been called in biblical times) was not accustomed to receiving thanks and adulation from those he served. Nor were his wages especially good. Jesus called us to be servants, not masters (Matt. 23:11). When our service is rendered without expectation of reward, our idealistic commitment will less likely become corroded.

Another quality of Jesus was his naturalness. He was always himself. There was never any pretense; he never wore a mask of hypocrisy to deceive others. He was a genuinely authentic man. Pretense is the deadliest foe of the Christian idealist. It can weary us as we try to remember which role we are playing at any given moment. When we are tempted to pretend to be something we are not, our idealism will suffer accordingly.

Another quality of Jesus' idealism was his willingness to let his idealism lead him to its ultimate consequences, which for him proved to be a Roman cross. He did not modify his course to protect himself or to make his life more comfortable.

Some Old Testament prophets experienced martyrdom because of their unyielding commitment to the purposes of God (Luke 13:34). They were people whose commitment to God was so complete that they proclaimed the Word of the Lord, regardless of personal cost or consequences.

They delivered God's messages of warning and judgment to their own people, though it grieved them to have to deliver such messages. But they also could speak messages of comfort and hope to those who would hear them. They believed that swords would be beat into plowshares (Isa. 2:4; Mic. 4:3) and that God would dwell in the midst of his people (Ezek. 43:1-5; see also Rev. 21:22; 22:3-5). They confidently proclaimed that the time would come when all peoples would stream to the holy hill of the Lord to acknowledge him as God and to worship him (Mic. 4:1-2; Zech. 14:16). They were both realists and idealists about their world—realists about the present age and idealists about what God was going to do.

Our own age seems to be obsessed with the ugly realities of things as they are. What we need is the idealism shared by the prophets that proclaims, "Behold, days are coming when . . ." (Jer. 31:31).

Notes

1. Ephraim was the name of one of the twelve tribes, but sometimes it was used to represent the Northern Kingdom of Israel. "Joseph" was also used in the same way (Amos 6:6; Ezek. 37:19).

2. Old Testament scholars seem more inclined today than formerly to acknowledge that the same prophet could and did preach messages of judgment and hope.

3. Matthew 16:18 has usually been interpreted to mean the Catholic Church or Peter's confession of faith. However, our Lord may have been employing a very subtle kind of irony and was saying: "Through the same kind of people as Peter—on such an unreliable, impetuous 'rock'—my church is going to be established!"

4. The KJV translation says "naughty figs," but this is archaic language. The Hebrew is literally "evil figs."

5. Many Old Testament scholars do not believe that these verses were originally from Jeremiah, but such conclusions are tenuous at best and largely unproductive. There is no valid reason why Jeremiah could not have announced a new covenant.

Bibliography

The books that have been written on Old Testament prophecy are innumerable. Those listed below are representative of studies that have been made of Old Testament prophecy. In addition to these sources, see also Old Testament introductions, theologies, commentaries on individual prophets, theological journals, and Bible encyclopedia articles.

Batten, L. W. *The Hebrew Prophet.* New York: The Macmillan Company, 1905.

Beecher, Willis Judson. *The Prophets and the Promise.* Grand Rapids: Baker Book House, 1905. Reprinted 1963.

Cornill, Carl H. *The Prophets of Israel.* Chicago: Opencourt Publishing Co., 1897.

Davidson, A. B. *Old Testament Prophecy.* Edinburgh: T & T. Clark, 1903.

Ellison, H. L. *The Prophets of Israel.* Grand Rapids: William B. Eerdmans Publishing Company, 1969.

Freeman, Hobart E. *An Introduction to the Old Testament Prophets.* Chicago: Moody Press, 1968.

Heschel, Abraham J. *The Prophets.* New York: Harper & Row, Publishers, 1962.

Hyatt, Philip J. *Prophetic Religion.* New York: Abingdon-Cokesbury Press, 1947.

Kirkpatrick, A. F. *The Doctrine of the Prophets.* London: The Macmillan Company, 1897.

Lindblom, J. *Prophecy in Ancient Israel.* Philadelphia: Fortress Press, 1962.

Mowinckel, Sigmund. *He That Cometh.* New York: Abingdon Press, 1954.

Orelli, C. Von. *Old Testament Prophecy.* Edinburgh: T & T. Clark, 1885.

Paterson, John. *The Goodly Fellowship of the Prophets.* New York: Charles Scribner's Sons, 1948.

Payne, J. Barton. *Encyclopedia of Biblical Prophecy.* New York: Harper & Row, Publishers, 1973.

Rowley, H. H., ed. *Studies in Old Testament Prophecy.* Edinburgh: T & T. Clark, 1957.

Scott, R. B. Y. *The Relevance of the Prophets.* New York: The Macmillan Company, 1944.

Wood, Leon J. *The Prophets of Israel.* Grand Rapids: Baker Book House, 1979.

Yates, Kyle M. *Preaching from the Prophets.* Nashville: Broadman Press, 1942.

Young, Edward J. *My Servants the Prophets.* Grand Rapids: William B. Eerdmans Publishing Company, 1952.